To: Dad with love from
Carolie xx
Christmas 1983

Up and Under

UP and UNDER

FRANK KEATING

A Rugby Diary

HODDER AND STOUGHTON
LONDON SYDNEY AUCKLAND TORONTO

Also by Frank Keating:

Caught by Keating! Sporting Quotations from the Seventies
Bowled Over! A Year of Sport
Another Bloody Day in Paradise!

Half-title: Norster goes up, Price (No. 3) gets under: but Wales still miss the ball against Scotland.

Title: New Zealand's mighty pack have delivered the ball again and Loveridge, the All Black's player of the series, set up another surge – in spite of Paxton's despairing charge. The only other British Lion in view is the flattened, burrowing, Price.

Designed by Margaret Fraser

British Library Cataloguing in Publication Data

Keating, Frank
  Up and under: a Rugby diary.
  1. Rugby football
  I. Title
  796.33'3'0924   GV945

ISBN 0-340-34508-X

Contents

Foreword

This is not a diary in the strictest sense. It is an enthusiast's half-year log in celebration of Rugby Union, a very good game for which I have had a passion all my life. After three long winter periods spent away from Britain following the sun and the England cricket team, I found I was missing some singular home comforts – one of which most certainly was the anticipation I had always felt as I twirled myself in scarves and woollies and set out to watch the Rugby Union internationals, those weekend pagan festivals held in five ancient capital cities and which rivet sportsmen each successive new year.

This journey finishes with the tour by the British Isles' Lions team to New Zealand, an irregular but definitively momentous challenge once or twice a decade and through which twines the history and spirit and very fabric of the game. Thus here is an attempt to hoard under one roof, as it were, a random collection of thoughts and fancies and fads that sum up my lifetime devotion for Rugby football, which was inspired first at school and then fostered in the clubs in the West Country of England.

As they say in Pontypool – 'Up and Under, Here We Go . . .'

Acknowledgments

More than most big-time international sports these days, Rugby Union continues to be first and foremost – and gloriously – a game for players, not hangers-on, and I must thank all those good fellows who have so generously spared me their time and stood me my beers. Also my press colleagues for their kindness (and their cribs!). Particularly I must thank the *Guardian*, especially its Rugby writer David Frost, sports editor John Samuel, both friends and enthusiasts, and Peter Preston, a likewise editor.

My thanks are also due to the book's editor, Richard Cohen, who has been particularly helpful and, as Mike Brearley remarked on another occasion, 'helpfully particular'; to Margaret Fraser, the designer, for organising Heather Laughton's immaculate typescript; to the one-and-only Gren Jones, Wales's and all Rugby's favourite cartoonist; and for collating some fascinating statistics that dot the text I am especially grateful to John Bale, the geographer, my *Guardian* colleague, David Irvine, and of course to Rugby's very own *Wisden*, the invaluable *Rothman's Yearbook*. Mrs Lysbeth Merrifield has compiled the excellent Index. Last but not least I would like to thank Neil Kinnock for his trenchant Introduction. A sparkling left-wing in the Clive Rees mould, he now spends his time coaching (at London Welsh) and watching (Newbridge and his beloved Cross Keys, both in his constituency).

Picture Credits: Those taken by Bob Thomas are on pp. 1, 2–3, 23, 28, 33, 54, 57, 87, 90–1, 113, 122, 123, 137, 156, 166, 167 (both), 169, 171, 172–3, 174, 175 and 176.
Those by Colorsport are on pp. 18, 35, 38–9, 45, 80 (both), 81 (both), 83, 89, 99, 111, 112, 114–5, 125 (both), 135, 140–1, 142, 148 and 151–2.
Those by the *Guardian* are on pp. 21, 43 and 98.
Those by John Darling are on p. 62.
That by Sporting Pictures (U.K.) Ltd is on p. 50.
That by the Press Association is on p. 51 and that on p. 16 is the work of Polly Breen, founder of the Douai Camera Club.

Introduction

Rugby is a game to love. In other sports an individual performance can give delight, slick play can earn respect, the rich mixture of instinctive skill and practised expertise can be joyous. In any sport tenacity, concentration, dexterity, inventiveness all earn roars from the crowd, muttered clichés of praise from the sages, shrugs of commendation from beaten opponents. Brilliance is brilliance wherever shown, whoever shows it.

But in Rugby the very shape of the ball makes cleverness an elementary condition of play. The deliberate necessity of tackling makes courage commonplace. Strength for shoving and stalling and reaching and running is not merely an attribute for occasional explosive use; it is a basic and continual ingredient.

In Rugby, the field of play is crowded. The formation for attack and defence is cavalry charge, line abreast. The target in open play must first be the man carrying the ball, only second the ball itself. Counter-attack – out of a tackle, a catch, an interception, or from robbery in line-out, scrum, ruck or maul – is the only sensible form of defence. And all that means that every one of the arts and sciences of speed, sidestep, switching, dummy passes, hand-offs, timing, kicking long or short, high or low, straight or sideways, supporting for continuity, security, recovery and fresh advance are built into this team ball-game as they are in no other.

That is the lovely Rugby that most try to teach and play and most want to watch. Even in a game which has a huge span of performance from dazzling perfection to hilarious and self-mocking hopelessness the ideals of fast, open play and controlled, organised might, of adult attitudes to refereeing decisions and of plain fairness, continue to rule.

Too often they have to strive to rule in spite of Thugby, a parasitic growth on Rugby Football that tries to excuse its sour, stupid brutality with banalities about 'a man's game', when all its sly savagery is the very opposite of anything recognisable as 'manliness'. It contaminates all levels of the game. No one deliberately invented it. Few will try publicly to justify it and even fewer publicly defend it. But it is nurtured at international and senior club level by an obsessive fear of losing, which often seems to overwhelm all other purposes of playing, including the desire to win by taking the reasonable risks of attack. It is accommodated at other levels of adult Rugby as a surrogate for skill, while in junior and even mini-Rugby the craze for victory at any price can strangle young talent and tutor youngsters in the negative villainies of intimidation.

Many – including the most illustrious names in modern Rugby – strongly and repeatedly condemn such violence. They are not being soft or soppy or pious. They know that in this physically hard and often furious game, if brutishness were ever regarded with complacency, let alone endorsed, all the sparkle would be terrorised out of existence, menace would replace ability, fellowship would be rotted by spite and Rugby would cease to be a sport.

There are other threats to the game, less frightening but equally serious and not entirely unrelated to the growth of violence. The problems come because Rugby Union lawgivers like to pretend that pure Corinthian values can reign in the age of Adidas and Patrick and Puma and Nike.

In the amateur game of Rugby Union leading players are expected to maintain standards of physical fitness equal to that of the 'Croesus-rich' stars of other sports, endure risks of serious injury, cancel normal family life, be the butt of any pot-bellied club Socrates or opinionated scribbler who chooses to needle them, depend upon the fortuitous goodwill or demanding patronage of employers who tolerate their absences. But when those players have pulled a £300,000 crowd to a stadium they still draw only derisory expenses. When they are paid for autobiographies or training manuals they join Beaumont, Edwards, Cotton, Mervyn Davies and many others as 'professionals' who cannot become coaches or selectors or be otherwise officially used in the Rugby Union game. Only the joke writers benefit from the mixture of anachronism and schizo-phrenia that brings the sporting excommunication of a player-turned-author by administering bodies which, at the same time, are obtaining sponsorship from a cigarette firm or concluding an exclusive contract with a sports-kit manufacturer.

It is five years since Gareth Edwards wrote, 'The Electricity Board does not care if you are in New Zealand having your head kicked in for the sake of the flag. They still send you the bills.' Since then nothing much has changed – although it is possible that the Electricity Board might alter their policy on charges for touring British Lions before the Home Union's change theirs on expenses. Meanwhile, ringmasters hover around the game with fat circus cheques and contracts. They are much more likely to be accepted by international players in their late twenties and early thirties and to damage the Rugby Union game if the administrators do not quickly amend their attitudes. They have to acknowledge that, whilst it is obvious that no international player is in the game for money, the financial losses together with the pettiness of rules that forbid earnings from writing or talking about Rugby Union take on a new significance when everyone knows that big money is now made directly and indirectly by those whose boots or booze or books are sold to and through the game.

Frank Keating is just the man to celebrate the virtues and damn the vices of Rugby. He is a moralist with a belly laugh, a mixture of memory man and polemicist, hero worshipper and idol toppler. In short – and in his own words – he is an 'overgrown schoolboy'. And anyone who thinks that to be a demeaning title should recall the encyclopaedic sporting knowledge of their own youth or listen to any youngster's understanding of right and wrong, fair and foul, an understanding that is not clouded by pomp.

With such qualities and enthusiasm Frank deserved better than the 1982–3 Rugby season for his return to writing about the game after cricketing winters abroad. There was good club and cup Rugby. But the Maori tour was disappointing, the international games – with two exceptions – varied from the dreary to the dreadful, and the Lions' tour seemed a miserable business for everyone.

The lonely death of Carwyn James in January 1983 was of a different order of misery, both for distant admirers of his perception and honesty, his intellect and gentility, like me, and for his close friends and workmates, like Keating. The sadness of his death is made more bitter by the knowledge that he was a prophet honoured everywhere save perhaps in the jealous, prissy parts of his own land.

The intuition and enterprise of a Carwyn is needed now in order to steer British Rugby out of its staleness. Crash-ball-set-up-the-maul has decayed from being a judicious prelude to a second attacking phase to a form of paralysis. Outside-halves aren't flying, they are perpetually kicking mortar shots for chasing forwards. Scrum-halves need to be built like – or at least feel like wing-forwards. Wings are on short time. Players are fitter and faster, they've played Rugby longer and are more thoroughly organised and coached than at any time in the history of the game. And yet (and I guard against distance lending enchantment) there seems to be less mobility, less fluency about so many games. Is squad training that becomes square bashing to blame? Is the prize of penalty points too generous by comparison with the reward for a try? Or has the tide of intimidation crept up far enough actually to forbid effective back play and to inhibit productive rucking and mauling? Surely – and I hope that my author host will permit the heresy – if galloping giants like the 1983 Australian Rugby League tourists can sparkle, Rugby Union can produce the same ability to move the ball without continual breakdown and the same convention of *always* (or so it seemed from the TV pictures of the tourists, as it seems with many top class League teams) taking the ball on the run. That must be the main means of attack in a handling game, as Carwyn James tirelessly insisted. But if the will to move the ball along the line is frozen by the domination of those who kick penalties and those who kick other people – the game will stagnate and the frustrations and risks grow. Now, when the danger is obvious but not yet complete,

Introduction

Rugby needs to give referees new powers of punishment for obstruction and late tackles and a penalty spot in the middle of the 22 as a new means of quick justice.

That is my pet antidote to negative Rugby. Everyone has one, of course; there is never any shortage of suggestions. We are all Rugby selectors, and any Members Bar could rewrite the Laws. The crowd in the National Stadium could sing the reforms – especially when the completed South Stand makes a huge chapel and voice tests are imposed on debenture buyers.

There is no shortage of players either. Among them there will be some with shining talents and fresh boldness of play – a little fitter, faster, with a more deadly kick or longer pass or dancing sidestep. And if someone will give them the protection of the Laws that take the jackboot out of the ruck those players will breathe fresh life into the game again. They always do. That is why Rugby is so alive, and so loved.

NEIL KINNOCK

CHAPTER ONE

An Old Obsession

I flew from London to begin my winter on a silvery-blue morning in early November. Not till the taxi from Toulouse airport had dropped me in the centre of a deserted old city did I realise that it was 11 November, Armistice Day. The French, overrun in two world wars, treat the very anniversary with a far longer solemn hush than the British with their nearest-to-the-date Cenotaph Sunday elevenses. The guidebooks *des vacances* may have Toulouse deep in the warm south but now, in spite of the sun, it was not a day to have left your muffler on an aeroplane. The city had not quite shut up shop for the memory. One or two bars were open. I snuggled up against a large russety cognac and an old steam radiator. It was exactly six weeks till Christmas. It was going to be the first full winter I would enjoy in Europe for four years.

The past three winters had been spent in the sun with the England cricket team. in 1980, six weeks in Australia on Mike Brearley's last tour; in 1981 I had been thrown out of Guyana with Robin Jackman and the rest of Ian Botham's team in the West Indies; and all last winter I perched on Keith Fletcher's rear mudguard as his MCC caravan lurched through India. That last had been a dreary cricketing exercise, though a rich and unmissable experience, but enough was enough – and anyway I was just a stopgap and the *Guardian* had discovered a fine new cricket writer to follow in the traditions of Cardus, Rowbotham, Arlott and Fitzpatrick in young Matthew Engel. Truth was, too, that I had missed the home fires burning and, as a bits-and-pieces sports freak, missed particularly the unique flavours of those cold and frosty fresh international rugby weekends when even those who don't know a corner flag from a traffic bollard or a prop from a clothes-horse get worked up about 'the match'. They are celebrations of big-time sport and small-time nationhood when, in turn, each of five ancient cities in just a 350-mile radius present, in their daft and differing and wholly original ways, a weekend carnival of comradeship and crunch and colour: when the whites play the blues play the reds play the greens. So here I was in Toulouse, drinking a warming cognac as aperitif to such a winter in prospect.

Mind you, we cricketing gypsies of the tropics were often mindful of such festivals back home. Two years before, in Antigua in January, I remember sploshing out of the blissful Caribbean with Chris Old, the England pace bowler and brother of Alan, the former England rugby fly-half. After stencilling our Man Friday footsteps across the sand to our beach hut, we spent an infuriating hour twiddling a transistor in an attempt to hear a BBC World Service report of the Wales v England rugby match at Cardiff. The crackle of static and the seashells in the ear relented for just the last few minutes. Woodward of England was an inch offside under his own posts and Wales had won. We relayed the news and the England cricket team groaned. From the back of the sunburned throng, I remember, that venerable eccentric, Don Mosey of the BBC, piped up, 'They didn't by any chance give the result of the Vale of Lune?' Mosey was thrown into the sea still wondering how his friendly little Lancashire club might have got on against, say, Fylde or Broughton Park.

Incidentally, Ian Botham, the captain of that shell-shocked band of ours in the West Indies, also likes his rugby. Well, he likes anything with a bit of passion to it. We had returned from Australia the winter before just in time to see the last of the rugby internationals. Bill Beaumont's England were going for the Grand Slam in Edinburgh. Ian came up with his father-in-law and Chris Lander, of the *Daily Mirror*, who had also been in Australia reporting the cricket. Bill's team laid waste Scotland on the field and, for two successive nights, our cricketing quartet laid waste the wine cellars of the North British.

Now I was to have a whole winter at it. Dozing in my pit that November morning before leaping about to get to the airport, I had listened to the early radio reports of England's latest cricket exploits in Australia. By coincidence 11 November was the very first day's play of the first Test match in Perth. Blofeld's bulletin came through loud and clear and as enthusiastic as ever, but I found myself surprised at not being the slightest bit *triste* to be duvet-huddling at home and not under an Aussie sun in splendour and shorts. Blearily I looked up my cuttings book: where was I exactly a year ago today? By fluke, with another man who liked his rugger. 'Bombay – Nov 11: Teatime at the Taj. It is 91 degrees, two degrees above normal for the time of year in Bombay. No mad dog's venture. Even the lolling English cricket team, the sun-tan oils dripping to drench their paperback thrillers, have long been driven to cover themselves in sodden towels and haul their beachbeds away from the poolside and into the castellated shadows of the renowned and stately old Taj Mahal Hotel.

'Inside, under whirring fans, genteel Indians sip their tea and mop their foreheads. Their eyes are hooded. Indeed at this time the rest of all India is taking its Sunday siesta in every patch of shade it can find all around the sub-continent. The beggars as well are on tea-break. Even the taxis have stopped hooting. But what's that? Yes, there it is again, a sort of familiar pocking noise. And to be sure, a mile or so away from the hotel, one exceptional Englishman is still daftly, devotedly at his work under the raging sun, still concentratedly poring over his labours and his love. He has a gang of sweating native apprentices lined up to toil in turn at his nod. More, he insists, and more again; and so the sweated labourers respond. Simply Geoffrey Boycott is having his second net of the day at Wankhede Stadium.

'The whole side had practised through the sweltering morning. Boycott had been first in for his twenty minutes, then lapped the perimeter of the vast ground a few times like a spring lamb. He had left his sopping gloves and thigh pads and chest protectors to dry on the grass in the hope of getting another knock before lunchtime. He looked pained when Bob Willis said there was no chance. "All right," said the ageing batsman like a spoiled schoolboy, as he gathered up his kit. "I'm coming at teatime, any road." And so he did. This eccentric Englishman and your humble mad dog returned to the teatime Taj together. "Your dedication, Geoffrey, is phenomenal," said I. "It is such it would have made you a star at any game you took up." He pondered long, then spoke: "Tell you what, if it hadn't been for cricket, I think I'd have made it at rugby union, y'know. I wasn't half bad at rugby at school. Full-back usually, but I would have been a bloody good fly-half if I'd had me way." And his sky-blue Coventry City-tinted contact lenses misted over at the thought of it.'

Now, for me, no more Boycott or Botham or Willis or Gower. For the next four months I would learn a whole new litany of loves and legends. And places, too, are just as evocative as the players and their deeds. Another marvellous fluke – as the Air France jet climbed out of Heathrow this morning and then tacked away southwards, I was on the right side to catch a glimpse down there of the very shrine itself. The Twickenham rugby ground stood silent, still and eerie in the late autumn sun. It was desolate and empty, an old pile sited midst serried suburban semis: it could have been what it seemed, a deserted ruin, a monastery unused for centuries: a relic of grander, more religious days.

It's the same in the summers when I might have been sent to cover, say, the cricket at Swansea or go on holiday to Pembrokeshire. The railway train from Paddington passes through Cardiff. As soon as the whistle goes for us to pull out west from Cardiff station I twitch expectantly and sometimes even have to go into the corridor for a blink-long flash of the Arms Park Stadium, its walls spearing into the sky from the very heart of the city like the towers of some medieval cathedral.

Again, especially on a lazy, bee-buzz blue midsummer's day, you can't adjust: can't quite remember what all the fuss was ever about. You've your *Wisden*, bucket and spade and sun-tan oil and it's hard to recatch the vibrations, to resummon the emotion you had when you were warmed by rugby on that cold and frosty day all those years before.

Twickenham and Cardiff . . . and Murrayfield too; and Lansdowne Road; and the jolly new Parc des Princes . . .

Twickenham, the High Church . . . green, green grass and faded green paintwork the colour of the cabbages Billy Williams's patch once gave its name to . . . celebrants all in white, polite claps for the chaps and decentish communion wine served from the Rover's boot in England's ritziest car park.

One year Peter Robbins, barnstorming favourite forward of my youth – as hard as nails but twice as difficult to hammer – recalled the lunchtime his own pre-match picnic was being upset by a nearby Rolls whose engine had been left running. The fumes were none too agreeable, so they asked the owner if he minded switching off. 'Not at all,' he replied, lifting the bonnet and wielding a corkscrew. 'I was just warming the claret.'

Robbins played a leading part in that coruscating Brace-Smith Varsity match of the middle 1950s. That was the second time we schoolboys had been crocodiled to Twickenham in our caps and scarves and borrowed sister's mittens. Memory of the first time a couple of years earlier excites me still as I write: England v New Zealand – and I was on the very touchline, I promise you, when a High Wycombe butcher called Ted Woodward carried on his back a marker called Jarden fully thirty yards, his hand-off palming thin air the while, before covering Black beetles engulfed them both.

I never saw New Zealand's winning try – away to the corner on my left – but I can recall, on that biting wintry day, how the frosty wisps of straw that kept blowing about did their best to divert the concentration of Bob Scott, bald as Brian Close and just as defiant, at full-back; he disdained the mark as he caught swirling skiers like Randall in the covers, then he'd kick a massive touch and grin like a half-guilty Typhoo monkey.

My first ever day at Twickenham had been in the middle 1950s. Brace and Smith for Oxford. Onllwyn at scrum-half, a jumping jack-in-the-box; intelligent Cambridge men, all with more than six O levels, would rush to

Douai Under 15s 1952. F.K. (scrum-half) extreme right, front row.

buy his dummies from twenty-five yards away; sometimes he'd pick up the ball from the heels of his pack and dart with it in a parallel line straight to the right touchline, but just before he was cooped up by light-blue hoops you looked across the field and saw the thing in the hands of the Oxford *left*-winger! Outside Brace, receiver of all the stolen goods, was M. J. K. Smith, wire glasses glinting with wry amusement at his friend's sleight of hand and foot. MJK was later to captain England at cricket, but ever since that December day at Twickenham I've always felt he kept his face straighter (as well as his punt down the line) than his bat. Cricketing, I've met Smith since but always revert to an embarrassed schoolboy's awe in memory of that afternoon. As I do with the mesmerising D. O. Brace with whom I come into friendly contact quite often in his role as Head of Sport at BBC Wales. Onllwyn thinks my face may be flushed with drink: in fact I'm blushing in the presence of one of the first sporting heroes I ever saw in the flesh.

Oftentimes too, when international fixtures have clashed, I fringe and cadge and hail-fellow around that car park while the duffelled English decant their plonk, and I close both eyes and think of Cardiff, for there I know all of a laughing sing-song will have broken loose: the city itself will be a jostling fairground; there no High Church, but Low Chapel: hellfire and red devilry, hymns and arias and brown brews out of cans, and Gren's *Western Mail* 'Special', and 'We'll win by at least twenty, boy, sure to,' and 'Anyone got a ticket spare?' and no corkscrewed decant but uplifting descant of Crimond and Cwm Rhondda . . . 'Feed Me Till I Want No More'. . . the tidal, tribal sound swells and swells again as the scarlet jinkers are willed once more to bring home the bacon to their ravenous congregation.

A different name now: the old Arms Park is the new National Stadium. But surely it's that same withered patch of grass near the touchline that has never recovered since my first visit there to see the mighty Springboks play the Barbarians in the early 1960s, when a Swansea sailor called Mainwaring (who doubtless worked in torpedoes) hit amidships a battle cruiser called Malan with a still unbelievably furious but fair shoulder charge. 'Look, no hands!' Malan's breath was concertina'ed from him – as was that of 60,000 other souls. There was a collective gasp for air, and I daresay still is when any two men who were there recall it. For all the legendary names in the daffy taffy lists that made up the outrageously good Welsh sides of comparatively recent years, I still curtsy a silent, awestruck genuflection to Mainwaring's square of scorched earth whenever I revisit Cardiff. He played only once for Wales. Nowadays I also manage to nod to that corner-flag where the immortal JPR, not so long ago, heroically muscled Gourdon into touch and allowed himself that momentary clenched-fist salute, like a boxer in his triumph.

Every square of green turf here has been marked off as Barry John's own purple patch. Gerald Davies too – sleeves rolled down, hands in armpits, shivering lonely as a corner-flag, but oh! when he was given the

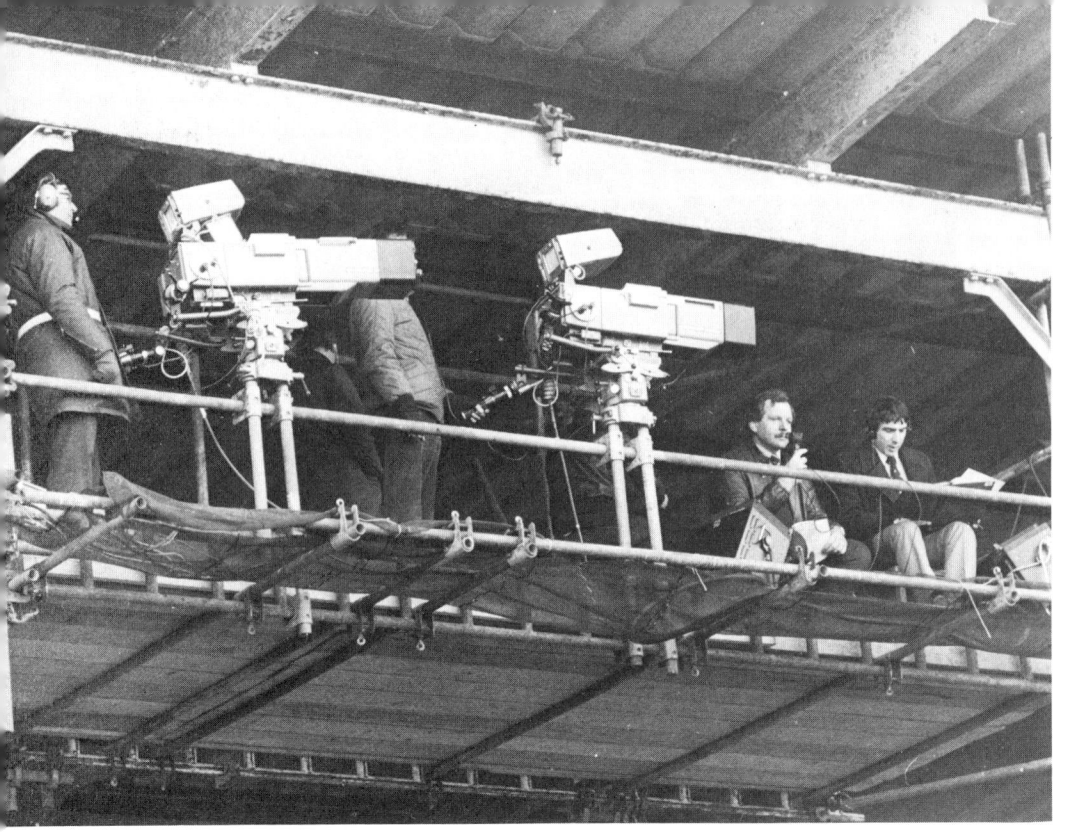

Box Pop . . . England would certainly miss their longtime totem and captain, Billy Beaumont, whose enforced retirement found him elevated to 'public figure' status – and to punditry on the rickety television gantries high above the international playing fields. Now he lends his weight, not to locking the scrum, but as sidekick to the BBC's Nigel Starmer-Smith.

---

ball . . . And Mervyn the swervin' . . . and, of course, Gareth Edwards. I remember, against Scotland one time, the shoulder-bunched boy in red definitely charging his way over from a five-yard scrum, festooned by dark blue, cursing Scotsmen. The power and the glory! Somehow that was more typical, more 'Gareth' than even, a few years earlier, his forty-yard dash for the Barbarians to decorate one of the finest tries ever scored – the run prefaced by Bennett's hopscotch, JPR's verve, Pullin's unlikely nerve, David and Quinnell's catch-and-take . . .

I'm afraid I always think of the Welsh too at Murrayfield, of Bennett's spring-skip in the sidestep and cuddle of the ball like a pillow at his cheek when he went over for that try; and, a few years earlier, of Taylor's greatest conversion since St Paul, when Delme couldn't look and Gareth had to commentate from the halfway line: 'He's running up . . . he kicks . . . it's high . . . it's straight . . . it looks good, Del . . . and by golly it's doing us good. It's over! Del, boy, we've won!' Then the whistle. Scotland 18, Wales 19.

The Welsh match always seems most specially special to Murrayfield. Ask anyone. The grey, gaunt city is awash with red by Friday teatime as dark little men wave tickets or doctor's papers; or both. Often it seems the 'North British' foyer could be the 'Angel's', lock, stock and barrelled up from Cardiff on an Inter-City weekend return. And on that always misty midday before The Match the visiting Celts are joined by men down from the hills with china-white Scandinavian complexions and pale knees below thick plaid skirts – as well as more clustering, mustering school-boys than anywhere else. And in the city's central bars another jar, a chaser, no? 'Just watch our Andy Irvine go!' And then that solemn walk to the ground in measured Episcopalian tread, faith and hope and may-the-best-team win, so that even the cocky swagger of the Welsh is unnerved. Murrayfield, Murrayfield, where I had to pull myself together to focus on the sight of Bill Beaumont being chaired off with his mythical Grand Slam after all those English years in the wilderness. And afterwards Bill actually said he was 'over the moon' – and I had to go behind the stand to be as sick as a parrot, for that was the teatime after the night before with England's other captain, Ian Botham.

But I had been awake enough earlier that day to applaud Rutherford's classic stand-off try and to wonder, when it happened, how old Bill McLaren had coped up there in his eyrie across the sloping acres. The hunk from Hawick ever determines not to let his heart rule his hurrahs by even the tiniest inflection when Scotland scores. I once wrote a verse to that effect – and, glory be, the *Guardian* went and published it – on the eve of the Welsh match at Murrayfield in 1979. It went, as they say, something like this:

> Tomorrow and tomorrow and tomorrow
> Keeps up his desperate tones from year to year,
> Trying to seem as neutral as he's ordered,
> But Scotland fail and agony is sheer.
>
> For big men do not weep in microphones.
>
> Stagg palms . . . wee Hastie gathers . . .
> Robertson to Frame upon the burrst . . .
> A crescendo that ever, too, was flattened,
> So we only *sensed* McCurses being currsed.
>
> For big men do not weep in microphones.
>
> How many times has expectation leapt
> Into his throat when Andy's on the ball,
> But then is strangled (like his cry!)
> By hordes of red, in ruck, set-piece or maul?
>
> For big men do not weep in microphones.
>
> But tomorrow! Oh, tomorrow! Oh, tomorrow!
> His Blues new bright with thistles prickly sharp,
> And Welsh uneasy (faded Scarlets now?)
> So when 'tis won tomorrow none at home will carp
>
> If Hawick's big man weeps with joy into his microphone.

An Old Obsession

By all accounts the Scots have been much improving since I've been away. Might this be the year for them – and McLaren – to give full throat?

Twickenham and Cardiff and Murrayfield . . . The enjoyably self-imposed brief of this diary is to cover a winter and summer of international rugby union – and this year, thank heaven, there is no doubt that I'll have to be journeying more than once to Ireland. They are the champions, after all. While my back was turned, cricketing in India, they won their first Triple Crown in a quarter of a century. Glory be!

Perhaps it's an Irish father. Or a boyhood among Benedictines. Or just that I was born to be best at home with the hearty fizz of expectation in Dublin before a match? At least rugby unites both Irelands for two weekends a year: when tragic North meets the sad South in genuine comradeship and love. One and all do then breathe sweet airs and Sweet Aftons and sink the black, to muse on Gibson the *nonpareil*, or 'Slatts', or the once precocious Ward, or his phenomenal successor, Seamus Oliver Campbell, or the day that the Kerry dancer's jigs were so ferociously performed – the day that Moss Keane almost beat (and beat up) the Welsh on his very own. Whatever he did that afternoon in 1978, Maurice Ignatius Keane did it to such an extent that, at the final whistle, Gareth Edwards himself flopped, appalled and weary, on to the dressing-room bench and put his head in his hands and knew an era was at an end and there and then his decision to pack it in was dragged from the secrecy of his gut to a confession on his lips. And, indeed, a fortnight later, Gareth retired. But what's this? They tell me Moss is still playing five years later and, to be sure, helped Ireland to their Triple Crown last winter. Will he still, in his 35th year, be causing mayhem through this new international season? We shall see.

The 1979 international against Wales – the last I saw before I went cricketing – was my first experience of rugby in Paris. I didn't know quite what to expect – but it was just what I expected! Friday night and Saturday morning in the 'Terminus', near St Lazare. Left Bank, Right Bank, and under the bridges of Paris, the Blues from the dusty South swapped bright red scarves and raised deep-red glasses in an exultation of the morrow. And once at the swank new concrete amphitheatre, fireworks and live cockerels and klaxons . . . and Clochemerle bands breaking out at every lull. *Allez, allez, allez, France!*

Four seasons ago the Welsh *allezed* like inspired frogs against France. But to no avail. Afterwards the door of the silent Welsh dressing-room was long barricaded, till John Dawes, the coach, stuck a sad nose out to say, 'some guys are nursing hard physical knocks, but mostly it is very badly dented pride.' Down the corridor, I remember, the French were

---

Carwyn James, who donated to a game an intellectual blend of romance and pragmatism. He warned about British rugby in the eighties. 'Most men just smell the wind; look out for those who create it.'

beside themselves. The place was like a first night foyer in the West End. Film cameras were showing them showering. When in doubt naked men just kissed each other and sought out the nearest microphone to tell of their part in the fête. Sisters and cousins and aunts were embracing their boys with joy . . . We've got it again, they all seemed to be saying, we've rediscovered ourselves.

In the evening the Welsh consoled themselves in unlikely corners. I poked my nose into the 'Winston Churchill' in the Champs Elysees – where Phil Bennett had once sung 'Swansea Town' with Sacha Distel on the night that J. J. Williams and Mervyn had run the bar – but the prices had trebled and there was not much jovial red around. It was indeed the end of an era.

The next morning I met Carwyn James for breakfast in a café near St Augustin. He had come up for the weekend on the sleeper from Italy with some of the players he coached at Rovigo. Italy. The finest *brain* the game had known was missionary now, giving freely of his talents to some extremely lucky, tyro Italians. Carwyn, with his blend of romance and pragmatism, remains a prophet round the world – but without honour in much of his own land. In his beloved, Welsh-speaking West he has long been canonised; eastwards, nearer the capital with its charcoal suits and Rotary clubs and envious, careful middle-class, he is regarded with suspicion. Such conformers do not take to non-conformist originals. Carwyn is a scholar. After playing with mesmerising Celtic skills for Llanelli, he coached the little club to unprecedented success through the 1960s, so much so that the British Lions appointed him their coach for the tour of New Zealand in 1971. No British Isles selection had won a series against the 'unbeatable' All Blacks in all the century. Carwyn's did – and with such high, wide handsomeness that the exhilaration of it broke the mould of umpteen deadpan, defeatist decades.

Carwyn was an occasional – and often brilliant – columnist for the *Guardian* so I recall I felt it allowable that morning in Paris to milk my friend's brain about England's next fixture against the rampaging French of the day before. We read first the Sunday newspapers. The local journalists' joy was unconfined. We didn't have to have much French to get the drift – '*Un pack château-fort . . . et un soupçon de fantaisie, un souffle de poesie de la part des baladins de l'arrière.*' So I ordered another Ricard (plus, of course, a gin and tonic for Carwyn: this chain-smoking, jinking little tub of a man travels the world, but never changes his style, his habits or his raincoats!) and pinned my ears back when I asked what mayhem this French side might cause England. Should they throw in the white towel now?

Not a bit of it, said Carwyn with certainty. 'The French hate playing at Twickenham, always have. England are bound to produce the goods soon. They just have to break out any day now. Much as I loved the French performance yesterday, they have a terrible weakness in the second row and the line-out that someone like Nigel Horton could expose

Another poacher turned gamekeeper. As prospective manager of the British Lions, the former rampaging Irish forward, Willie-John McBride, spent this winter in the stands, auditioning over sixty players for his team to tour New Zealand in the summer. As the Championship unfolded, the task looked increasingly difficult.

something rotten. For all the panache of the French yesterday, didn't you notice that they were using two or three men line-outs? If that isn't a confession of a terrible weak link what is? Honestly, I can see Horton destroying them at Twickenham unless they do something about it.'

A week later the England selectors did choose Horton, summoned up the beanpole who used to be a Midlands policeman and who then ran a bar in this very same city of Toulouse . . . and, a fortnight later, Horton duly beat the French on his own at Twickenham. You could never argue with Carwyn. You just had to sit at his feet and listen – and invariably it would come to pass.

I wondered even if Carwyn might pop up here in Toulouse this week. He was far easier to bump into by accident a million miles from home than to reach on the telephone at his Carmarthen village house or Llandaff flat – as his sister and telephonist, Gwen, would testify.

Carwyn was aware I was embarking on this rugby journal, and with typical generosity had promised encouragement, advice and steerage. Now I was keen to log his first thoughts, not only on immediate matters in Europe but even on what were to be the book's final chapters – the British Lions' tour to New Zealand far away in the summer. No man was better qualified to fill me in – even here in Toulouse on Armistice Day – on the men, the manners and the modes that would be worth watching for till March when Willie-John McBride, the manager, and Jim Telfer, the coach, were given their side – a dozen years after Carwyn's flamboyant and now legendary Lions had run ragged the famed All Blacks for the only time this century.

CHAPTER TWO

Opening Skirmishes

Meanwhile, in Toulouse for the first of my winter's skirmishes: France v Argentina. And, alas, sad evocations of a far more tragic battle – one with real bullets – that had taken place but six months before on the Falkland Islands. The War of Galtieri's Cheek, and Thatcher's Nerve. It was worthwhile being here if only to tell a group of Argentine international rugby players that many men in Britain mourned with equal grief the lives of every young soldier, from either side, in that mad, Maggie month of May. It was further appropriate somehow that I had come to them in Toulouse on Armistice Day.

It was sharply cold as I walked the city, but a serenely still, late afternoon halo remained. The leaves remained on the trees, but very few people were in the streets. Old ladies wore black hats and all was tranquil and reflective. The flame at the Cenotaph Arc was as bright as the wreaths of flowers and now the temporary stands stood empty in the sparkling sun after the morning's Armistice parade. It was rather like the deserted set an hour or two after shooting had finished of the climax of that shuddering film *Day of the Jackal*. But this was not a day for jackals.

It might have been up in Dax where, after the morning's sombre services, doubtless the town was allowed *en fête* to see the Argentine tourists beat the French Barbarians XV by 22–8. This evening the Argentines would arrive in Toulouse and, in three days' time, on Sunday, they would play the full French national side – and my winter would have begun. It was a short tour and would finish with another international in Paris next weekend. So far, by all accounts, the visitors had made a bitty start to their trip, playing hot and cold, fast and loose, in almost the traditional manner of their hosts. They opened with a glorious 38–15 win against a French Selection, but then lost a return match to the same side, 25–15. And the previous weekend the Bataillon de Joinville XV – the military academy where many of France's good sportsmen do their national service – had beaten them 27–9.

Next morning, for old times' sake, I attempted to read the newspapers in Toulouse's gracious old centre, at the Café Donjon, which used to be owned by that same Nigel Horton, the former fuzz, the line-out lank whom Carwyn had forecast would beat the French on his own those few years ago before I went cricketing. The papers seemed full of *'Exclusif: Princesse Diana, elle veut un nouveau bébé.'* But inside they were fuller of *le rugby*. Each rag seems to have at least four rugby specialists, analysing and dissecting, disputing and demanding. On top of the locals, the French have their national sports paper, *L'Equipe* and, down here, another daily that seems to cover only rugby, *Midi Olympique*. Apparently, the day before in Dax, the Argentines had played the classic tourists' game – defending with well-drilled stubbornness against the early verve of the pick-up side before cutting loose with their more practised moves when the Barbarians ran out of steam and cohesion. As one local paper put it: *'L'équipe Argentine commence remarquablement en defense, et après Hugo Porta, et ce n'est pas nouveau, faisant le reste.'*

Ah, Hugo Porta. I ordered another *café au lait*, then telephoned the Argentinians' hotel just out of town and made a date to meet Señor Porta. The headline on the report had said, simply, 'Toujours Porta'. Many say he is the grandest, most consummate fly-half in the game today. It will be good to meet him – and intriguing to talk too with the man with one of the grandest names in the world: the Argentine tour manager is called Rodolfo O'Reilly. Perhaps Sr O'Reilly will turn out to be a descendant of the very earliest South American players who went over, as engineers and navvies, from Ireland and Scotland to build the Argentine railways more than a century ago? The first recorded rugby union match between these homesick Celts was in May 1874 at the Buenos Aires Cricket Club in Palermo Park. By the by, the first non-English team to challenge the original British pioneers was formed in 1904.

Of all the 'emergent' rugby-playing nations Argentina has probably the strongest and longest lasting rugby links with Britain. In 1910 England's missionary international, J. E. Raphael, took the first British side over to play and beat 'The Natives of Argentina'. The Argentines are now a fully-fledged and dangerous international side, whatever the edict of the paternal and anachronistic fixtures secretary at Twickenham. I remember the ever-bruised, ever honourable Bill Beaumont returning from England's tour there a couple of years ago and saying something to the effect of, 'make no mistake, a cap against Argentina is a cap very well won and absolutely the equal as far as I'm concerned of one awarded against Wales, Ireland or even New Zealand.'

I went to watch the Argentines training. *Si*, Señor O'Reilly, a beaming, roly-poly, well-heeled former prop-forward presumes his ancestors must have come across the sea from Ireland in the last century – certainly he remembers once drinking all night to the memory of it in a dingy bar in County Cork with Tom Kiernan on his only visit back to the land of his fathers. He winces at the memory, guffaws expansively, introduces me to Hugo Porta, and leaves us alone – with the warning to steer clear of politics.

By way of 'research' all I had to go on was a dog-eared cutting of Carwyn James's from the *Guardian* of the day he had seen Porta play for the South African Barbarians against the British Lions at Durban in 1980. For a month I was on that tour, but missed that exhibition. This is what Carwyn wrote:

'I shall not easily forget Hugo Porta's studied performance yesterday at Kingspark's cosy, colourful setting on a hot and humid late afternoon. It was fitting too that he should have been watched by Barry John and Phil Bennett, the king and prince of fly-halves in the 70s. The mantle of the one or the other hung easily on Hugo Porta's broad shoulders. The Lions who did so were privileged to play against him. His all-round display revealed the lack of class and skill in the play of the Lions on this tour and that of the Springboks in the Tests. A Porta on either side would have decided the series. To study the craftsmanship of a great player is a privilege. At the set and the loose scrums Porta varied his positioning in such a way that he used the length of Ian Buchanan's pass to the best advantage by varying his angles of running. Sometimes he would stand within breathing distance of him either to bring Mark Loane, the No. 8 and fellow tactician, into play or else to run in and arc before straightening the threequarter line with a fall-away pass. His varying lines and his occasional tumbling, loping running rather bemused the Lions' back row who thought that they had him covered but found that they could not lay a hand on him. Porta, like Barry John, can carry a painful and at times disinterested facial expression which tends to lull the opposition into a mistaken sense of security . . .

'For Hugo Porta rugby football is a running and handling game, and he regards it as a minor art. His line kicking is meticulously measured and weighted, and hardly a yard is wasted as the ball finds touch . . .

'There are so many ways of watching a match. Yesterday afternoon ten minutes of play convinced me that, whatever the drama, the hero of the main plot would be Porta and that whatever happened in the sub-plot would be contested at a much lower level of skill and intellectual awareness. At the after-match function I was delighted to hear Ollie Campbell and Gareth Williams, the open-side flanker of the day, paying glowing tributes to the play of the master. It was like watching the unhurried stroke-play of a Barry Richards at Lord's or Graham Pollock at the Wanderers. It was like watching Borg at Wimbledon.

'For a critic or a coach or a former fly-half it was a question of having one's faith restored in the aesthetic and artistic possibilities of backplay which have deteriorated so drastically all over the world during the last years of a dying decade. The Lions failed in that task. Hugo Porta, bless him, did not.'

Now, two years on, in a hotel outside Toulouse, he seems keener to talk politics than rugby football. Hugo Porta wears the trim, tailored black

The facial expression that tends to lull the opposition into a mistaken sense of security. Off the field, Hugo Porta is sombre, serious and courteous: on it, insouciant and puckish, yet with a knowing aura about all he does.

blazer of the Argentine touring team. His hairstyle is as neat and tidy and precise as his manner; he is sombre, serious and courteous; he looks like the lawyer he is and, on this day, the only clue to his hobby is a vicious, horizontal two-inch gash of congealed blood on his right cheekbone.

I told him I didn't know, couldn't guess at, how long there would be an unwritten insistence in Britain that they should not play games against their South Atlantic 'enemies'. He was 31 now, he said, and there was not much time left for him. 'I would love desperately to play one more match there with my friends in Britain.' The Falklands factor, I told him, had destroyed more than football, and he should realise that only this week, Ray Williams, secretary of the Welsh Rugby Union, said, 'Wales are due to tour the Argentine in 1984. The Welsh Guards lost a lot of men in the war, and such a visit would be an emotive issue, to say the least.' Why, asks Porta, his sad brown eyes pleading for agreement, why are sportsmen dragged into politicians' disagreements? Last week, the French Barbarians XV invited the former England full-back, Marcus Rose, to play against the Argentinians. Porta's side, to a man, he says, were overjoyed that Rose turned up. 'Before the game I go to Marcus and shake his hand and say, "Thank you for coming, it has made us most happy." And afterwards we all have a long talk with him and we say many things together and we realise how idiotic it is that this "war" could even destroy one friendship.'

Mercifully, says Porta, none of the Argentine side was called to take up arms. But many friends from his sports club in Buenos Aires and from his De La Salle monastery school did have to fight. 'By good fortune none was killed. But we were frightened for them and we prayed every night for their safe return. It was a war between governments, between Mrs Thatcher and our President, not a war between young men who have been pleased to call themselves dear friends.' He gestured. 'Sport must be placed here, and politics over there; they must always be kept separate. How futile, anyway, to kill people over two ridiculous pieces of land in the middle of the sea.' At school, Porta played soccer – 'No. 9 or No. 10, of course,' he smiles. Many said he should turn professional. 'But my father insisted I should study. I agreed with him. At my club they play all sports. Rugby was fun. At first I was scrum-half, then in 1970 I was selected for national training. I was fourth-choice scrum-half. Then one day all the fly-halves were injured – they chose me.'

Now I was looking forward with even more relish to the match. Perhaps Porta would find some room to manoeuvre against the French, for the home side would be playing a reserve back row on account of injuries to their usual trio, led by that exhilarating blond hunting terrier, Jean-Pierre Rives, who had badly injured his knee playing in the first Barbarians' match against the tourists the previous week. The other two famed musketeers who hunted with their captain, Joinel and Rodriguez, were also hurt. Even after only a day or two down in the rugby-loving south one is overwhelmed by the passion for rugby – as well as by the annual, brooding uncertainty as to how the French team will turn out for the new season.

The previous week the French A side had been beaten by the Russians, of all people, so there was still weeping and gnashing amongst the rugger fraternity. After the defeat one of the French selectors, André Moga, said, 'The vintage of our rugby in France at the moment is about five per cent proof, and if you dilute that three times you would burst your bladder without getting a hangover.' Ah me, *c'est la vie*. But I daresay it will be looking much more *rosé* by the end of the weekend.

Mind you, not too large a crowd is expected for the match. Although these plains before the Pyrenees have always been the hot-bed of French rugby they do not apparently pack them in for the international games. Here the club sides take precedence for spectators – Toulouse itself, and Tarbes and Lourdes, in fact all along the line from Beziers to Biarritz. Two or three times a season, however, they go to Paris for the international – berets, cognac in the case, live cockerels in the luggage rack, and *La Marseillaise* in full throat.

Rugby first reached the French from Britain via the Channel ferries. Le Havre, in the north, reckons to be the oldest club, founded in 1872 by a Mr Longstaff, the Southern Railway's agent there. Then the game, played initially by resident Brits in the wine trade ports, seeped down the west coast. The first France v England international was played in Paris on 22 March 1906. England won 35–8. The 'French' team was captained by one G. Lane, a Welshman who worked in Paris and was a member of the all-purpose Racing Club. The full-back and inside-centre were, respectively, W. H. Crichton and E. W. Lewis, both Englishmen who worked in Le Havre. The wing-forward was a former Chicago US football player, A. H. Muhr. The rest of the team were young Parisians whose main sport was either soccer, athletics or tennis.

The Parc des Princes has been rebuilt twice since then. On that day the officials' little stand was decorated in purple and gold for the reception of the British Ambassador, who, alas! was unable to attend, 'urgent business' having arisen. Three thousand watchers, however, turned up, 'preferring', says a report, 'the healthy emotions of the match to the jostling and so-called pleasures of the boulevards'. There was a running commentary on the play in *L'Auto*, the leading sports paper of those days: '4.9 p.m. – Uproar. We frantically wave hats and sticks. Has a mid-Lent procession of beauty queens been sighted? No. France has scored. 4.21 p.m. – another English try. We are now hardened to pain . . .' But it was 'a sensational match and an historical day. The English were great strapping chaps. The French second-half display encouraged hope for the future.' The same reporter referred to the presence of spectators of the so-called weaker sex. Then *Le Figaro*, which did not mention the ladies, unconsciously atoned in its account of the play by saying that 'a violent wind deranged the most beautiful combinations'.

By then, too, the south had taken its first sniffs of rugby's flavours. It was never to lose the scent. The influence of two Welshmen was crucial. From opposite ends of the Pyrenees they spread the same gospel. At Bayonne, a Penarth rugby nut called Owen Roe, who had seen the Welsh beat the All Blacks at Cardiff in 1905, decided to coach his local club. And across the great mountain range, from Bayonne's Atlantic to the Mediterranean of Perpignan, another Welsh exile, Rowland Griffiths, was elected captain of his adoptive rugby club on 1 January 1912 – exactly forty years to the day that Jean-Pierre Rives was born in Toulouse.

The southern French were eager and quick to take to the game. The two Welshmen, Roe and Griffiths, had both been inspired from home by witnessing the first 'golden era' of Welsh rugby when, of a sudden, the Celts had grafted the joys of threequarter play on to the ponderous, he-man's game the English public schoolboys had taught them a quarter of a century before. Roe's Bayonne club was only founded in 1906, yet half a dozen years later Roe was taking his team to play in the national cup semi-final against the mighty Bordeaux, which had long been established as a club, sponsored by the wine trade Anglos. Bordeaux had won the final eight times, indeed had never lost a cup match at home.

Bayonne's sparkling back play was a revelation. They won 9–0, then travelled up by *wagons lit* to Paris itself to meet the Universitaire de France at the Parc des Princes. The Parisians laughed at the minnows. It was like Crewe Alexandra getting to Wembley. But Bayonne won by 33–8, with Roe himself playing a leading part. That Sunday in Paris in April 1913 marks the beginnings of the modern French game. The south had taken rugby to their hearts – the more so when a year later that other missionary and latter-day Carwyn James, Rowland Griffiths, took his Perpignan side to the 1914 final, and the men from the mountains again gave the capital a glittering display.

Now, almost seventy years on, the French from the south – only two consistently leading sides, the Racing Club and the University, come from Paris – continue to play the refreshing, improvised game their grandfathers learned from Roe and Griffiths. And on to the spontaneity and colour they have attached a discipline and hardness. They are demons for coaching. Not that much rugby is played in schools. The club is all, and even the smallest village club might have an under-12 side. On the other hand, the social side is very different. You go to the club for *le rugby*, not for *le booze-up*. That fine former British international, Roger Shackleton, knows the French well and once explained, 'The traditional French rugby club has developed in a very different way to its counterpart in Britain. Every French club is a direct reflection of the interests of the municipality in which it is based – what is good for the team must reflect well on the town, they say. So very strong links have been forged between clubs and local councils, to the point where most clubs play on municipal stadia (surrounded by running tracks, netball courts, tennis courts and soccer pitches) and are visibly financed to a great part by grants from the local councils. In this situation, very few clubs have developed social facilities of any permanence at their grounds, and rely on the support of a local bar to provide their meeting room and bar facilities. Rugby in France provides a forum for individuals to express themselves – players, presidents, selectors – but does not have the inherent social fabric around it that the game in Britain has developed.'

Without such a fabric, French club rugby has not achieved sufficient stability to have the confidence to allow free movement of players. Not that there is any professionalism in the actual sense of wages; but there is, as in Wales, a feeling that to be a leading rugby player in France you have the cream of any local 'situations vacant'. Thus self-interest dictates that players move not for family or work reasons but to further their 'careers' directly. To combat this, the movement of players between clubs, usually premeditated, is now controlled to such an extent that players moving clubs are essentially banned for a season from first team rugby.

Jean-Pierre Rives is a recent victim of this situation. In the summer of 1982 he left Toulouse, where previously he had worked in the law courts, and moved to Paris to join the drink firm of Pernod, the national beverage. The rules stopped him playing first team rugby for a year in the capital and he was even threatening, I heard, to fly to London each week to play for the Harlequins. I would find out tonight for, in spite of his gammy leg, Rives had returned to his beloved home town for the match. So on one and the same day I would have had the pleasure of being in the presence of the two most charismatic players in the world game. Well, who else had seen it all and done it all, and could also speak out fluently over the whys and wherefores? Offhand, only Graham Mourie of New Zealand and perhaps Andy Irvine of Scotland would come remotely into the same bracket. It is interesting that neither Rives nor Porta is British; but both represent the Corinthian ethos of honourable sportsmanship that so fired the founding fathers of modern team games, those muscular Christians who prayed and played together in the public schools of Victorian England.

Rives had lunched with his deputy as French captain, the scrum-half, Gerald Martinez, another Toulousain. Martinez had captained the French B side against Scotland B as long ago as 1975 – the very match that Rives had sprung to prominence and won the first of his many rave notices. He is in his late 20s, with frizzy brown hair, spectacles and a ready smile, but he has the enquiring open face of a first-year student as he sits, plotting for the morrow, in a café surrounded by friends.

Jean-Pierre Rives, by comparison, looks like an ageing student trendy, an extra from a remake of *The Wild Bunch*, but in which Gucci might have been the designer: sky-blue patent leather jacket and posh gym shoes with an ochre flash to match his cascading hair of Pernod-yellow. The writer Geoffrey Nicholson once said that at the very least he should be the figure who appears below the balcony as the lady steps out of her Badedas bath. He has battle scars on his cheek and forehead. The only other clue to his hobby is the invitation to bend down and feel his knee and see how

The wispy, corn-stoop hair is a rallying beacon for the game's romantics. Jean-Pierre Rives at the eye of the storm . . . 'excitement all round, movement, an atmosphere that sets you quaking, stands your hair on end; you are struggling to keep your inner balance in the middle of a tempest.'

puffed and swollen it is. In recent years he has become the totem of French rugby – and not only French rugby. The wispy, corn-stoop hair has been a rallying beacon for the game's romantics the world over. His courage is legendary, as is his chivalry. He has played tough and furious, and hates to lose, but if he does he says 'Bravo!' He rabbits too much to referees, but he says that's a language problem.

Rives is thinker and tearaway at the same time. Like Porta, he has no family heritage of rugby. His ancestors are from middle-Europe; he spent much of his childhood in black Africa, where his father worked. He took up rugby at fifteen because he was not as good as he thought at his beloved tennis. He would like to have been Bjorn Borg. He once played the Swedish *nonpareil* and says he went on to court 'presuming I was going to beat him'. He lost 0–6, 0–6.

Like Porta, Jean-Pierre also talks of war – but only in the abstract. He speaks a slow, precise, philosopher's pidgin English. 'Someone once said that if you want to interest a Frenchman in sport you tell him it's war; and if you want to interest the British in a war you persuade them it's a game. Whatever the truth in that, the whole point of rugby is that it is, first and foremost, a state of mind, a spirit . . . it has a remarkable confraternity. People talk the rugby they love; the game's very name is a magic word. People identify with the rugby group. All this must be preserved and promoted. From the beginning of time, people have been killing each other in the name of a group – tribe, fatherland, whatever. The rugby group is founded on other laws, and on a different spirit.'

He feels that sometimes in France they think that the 'real' rugby is out in the sticks, in the small local communities and villages. He is a federalist. Everything must bend for the health of all France. 'The quality of the national side determines the level of rugby's appeal throughout the country. There should be no opposing village and national games. Any sport is a pyramid whose base and apex are absolutely complementary. If they love the game, it is the duty of all players and officials at whatever level to endeavour to produce a thrilling national side.'

A year or two ago Rives enlivened the game's invaluable statistical bible, *Rothmans Yearbook*, when, out of the long grey slabs of facts and figures, leaped his romantic's view of playing at the topmost level. Pressure? *Sûrement, c'est magnifique*: 'I disagree that pressure at the top removes the pleasure for the players. Now there is certainly no denying the pressure to play well for your country and for the game itself. The pressure is important in itself; without it, international play would be cheapened. And the pressure is part of the pleasure. There is fear of not playing well. The fear heightens the occasion by increasing the difficulty, but it is great pressure that makes the great match.'

Rives says he cannot conceive the possibility of a great match being played behind closed doors. To him an international game is 'excitement all around, movement, an atmosphere that sets you quaking and stands your hair on end'. The struggle, he says, is in keeping one's inner balance

The colourful Blanco usually flew highest . . . At last the French selectors dared choose the aircraft worker from Biarritz as an attacking full-back. Twice each game at least, he electrified the matches he played in.

in the middle of a tempest. It is no ordinary experience – 'there are great heights to reach (and abysmal depths, if it comes to that), and dreams to dream.' One takes the field believing one is strong, so great is the honour of representing one's country. Enthusiasm, too, is vital, and he talks of the boy who sits down at his piano and dreams he is a little Mozart. 'Dreaming is part of enthusiasm, which also resembles faith.'

It was still sharp and nippy and a keen wind got up after the watery afternoon sun had soon buried itself in the mists down there over the Pyrenees. France took a long time to warm themselves and us, but once they realised they had the measure of the Argentines they ran out easy winners, 25–12. The visitors had led 9–4 at half-time, but even then one gave them very little chance of holding on to the reins. Blanco, the French full-back, was everywhere, while the two wingers, Sella and Esteve, were running like March hares. The French scored four tries to Argentina's one, and in an increasingly rampant second-half the home side gave ominous notice that, with tails up, they could easily double such a score when the teams met again in Paris the following week – and that they could well field a formidable Championship side when sterner matters got under way in the new year.

Opening Skirmishes

Argentina flattered themselves early on but even they could not have been deceived as they held a 9–0 lead through often desperate defensive blocking and tackling. The referee, the Irishman, John West, conducted the game with flair and an understanding of flow and advantage. At first this suited the galumphing, less sophisticated Argentinians – always excusing Porta, who started with his customary élan, but as the game went on he was almost back on his heels in despair. There were a couple of delicious little chips early on, and one half-break that had the cover melting. Always, in that first half-hour, there was an insouciant, puckish but knowing aura about all he did. Then, behind his beaten pack, he saw less and less of the ball, certainly never going forwards.

Just on half-time France opened the bottle of fizz. They continued to sparkle – if often wastefully – for the following forty minutes. First, the fly-half, Camberabero, son of his famous, hoofing father, who had hitherto shown even more faith than dad in line-kicking, lifted a tantalising lob, going right, and dropping on the very line. The Argentine left-winger, Varone, waited under it an age till it was snatched from under his nose by his opposite number Sella, who triumphantly tumbled over. The siege was as good as finished. France moved up some gears. First came the try of the match: a long line-out ball gave Chadebech a half-break, his fellow-centre Mesny speared through and the wing Esteve went over. Next, a penalty by Blanco put the French in the lead, and though Porta restored the Argentines' position briefly with an answering bazooka the home side were unstoppable: a penalty and a drop goal by Camberabero were decorations on tries by the high-stepping Blanco – who hands off with his knees – and by Sella. At the very last, Porta missed a penalty under the posts – and promptly fell back on to the ground in anguish. He took a long time to get up.

At the banquet that evening the Argentine champion was once more his trim, charming self. He made a gracious speech of which I understood not a word, but which was interspersed with regular 'amigos'. The French stand-in captain, Martinez, responded, calling the whole visiting side 'héroique' and their captain 'le special de mundo' and 'sportifitie exemplaire'. Then the Argentine coach, the tubby Sr O'Reilly, stood up and started singing something that sounded very much like the processional hymn down the road at Lourdes, 'Ave Maria'. Rives briefly looked in, still in his sky-blue leather jacket and snazzy plimsolls, while I was able to chat to Porta, who now sat quietly as the songs went on with a harmony and class one would never get at this time after a rugby match in Britain. Meanwhile the local Sunday sports paper was starting to roll off the presses. In it there was joy unconfined at the French victory and also a tribute to Porta in the newspaper's editorial:

> 'Porta est un symbole, un chèf, le maestro du carousel, l'homme aux pieds d'or, le bon génie de la Pampas celui qui a donné au rugby Sud-Americain ses lettres de noblesse . . . il donne une merveilleuse sensation d'équilibre et de sérénité ce qui représente, à ses yeux, cette "vuelta" dans l'hexagone.'

Better even than the *South Wales Echo* on Barry John! Porta never saw John play, but he had watched him on film and been enchanted. You mention Gareth, and his eyes glint and he shakes his head in wondrous recollection. He has no doubt about the two most fierce but fair wing-forwards who have marked him. The former French flanker, Skrela, and his apprentice – 'that gentleman over there, Jean-Pierre Rives. If he is not tackling you he is always hounding you, worrying you, leading the charge for his country. He is so fast and energetic, so chivalrous and so proud.'

It was comparatively early. Porta went to bed. Rives was off with his cronies. Martinez took some of his team to his uncle's bar near the railway station. Champagne flowed, with cognac chasers. The two great prop forwards, Robert Paparemborde and Pierre Dospital, sang haunting Basque shepherds' songs. Paparemborde is probably the best tight-head prop in the world. He is six feet exactly and weighs just fifteen and a half stone but his presence is more massive than that. He does not speak English but, off the field, transmits a quiet friendliness – even to visiting Englishmen. Bob Donahue, an American journalist based in Paris who has become passionate about European rugby, half commentated and half translated: 'Paparemborde was nicknamed "Patou" because a dog always waited for the boy outside school, and *patou* is Béarnais for doggie. Up in Laruns, a town of sixteen hundred not quite twenty-five miles south of Pau, the parents still speak Béarnais. It was Robert's first language, unless you count these lyrics. He speaks even faster than the average Frenchman. His conversation is known for its entertaining sagacity: Parisians call him a sage. He can keep his tongue or speak his mind, almost always with humour in the eyes. Non-French names are pronounced correctly: Lynch, for instance, the Irish prop, whom he's watched closely on television. "He made it hell for the bloke opposite. It was impressive." When the twinkle fades it is usually straight into sleep.

Paparemborde was an all-round athlete, with representative honours in handball before he played in his first rugby match, at the Pau Lycée, aged seventeen. He had come down to the lycée from his valley, where his father was a road-mender. Within months the youngster was in the senior side of the Section Paloise, never to leave it. The very next season he propped in a schoolboy international against Wales. A black belt in judo did no harm to his confidence – or his balance. He binds by the laws and shoves straight, but the slope of his shoulders and the strength and craft of his scrummaging are such that he beats his man and bedevils the opposition's hooker.

Patou sang on. Joining in the choruses, life and soul of the party, was a young man who, all his colleagues were telling me, could have as big an influence on France's performance in the coming Championship as Paparemborde himself. Serge Blanco is twenty-four, a dusky, lithe six-footer. With his liquid stride and exuberant confidence he put me in mind of the most mesmerising and fluent athlete I have ever seen – the Cuban

'Papa Patou' signs off. Even his most competitive and grudging opponent would admit Paparemborde the best tight-head prop in the world. The Frenchman's ambition was to be invited, just once, to play for the British Barbarians. He was asked, on one occasion – but the game was cancelled. Here he plays the final match of his career – for the Baa-baas at Murrayfield. At the finish the strong man from the mountains left the field with tears of emotion – and gratitude.

quarter-miler, Juantorena. He was born in Caracas. His father was Venezuelan but, on his death when the boy was two, Blanco's mother returned to her native Biarritz.

So committed is Blanco to attack and to carefree unorthodoxy that for the two seasons he has played for France the selectors have funked putting him at full-back – his club position at Biarritz – and played him on the wing. His first cap in the international championship, against Wales two seasons ago, he scored a try from the first pass he received. He was on the right wing: he scored after taking the pass outside the *left* wing! This afternoon the selectors had had the daring at last to play him at full-back. What glories might we be in for?

Sure enough, the following week in Paris, in the second international against Argentina, Blanco by all accounts electrified the game with a magical sixty-yard dash to give France victory 13–6. As in Toulouse, the tourists made a good fist of containing the French for three-quarters of the match. Again the French came late, a riveting winger's try putting them ahead just after the hour; then Blanco's coruscating counter-attack, after poor Porta had kicked ahead and found no support, set off the klaxons and the November fireworks with just five minutes remaining. The French seemed in the trim. Across the Channel, the four British sides were easing into their rhythms and candidates for the trial matches were being either rubbed out or pencilled in. There were eight weekends before France's first match – against England at Twickenham. Blanco and his backs had sounded their warning. And Jean-Pierre Rives was getting fitter by the day.

"...AND SO GENTLEMEN, AS WE SAY IN SPORTING GOODS CIRCLES – CHECKMATE!"

CHAPTER THREE

Seeing Things in Black and White

The day before I had seen the French fire their warning in Toulouse, Wales had coldly and efficiently beaten the New Zealand Maoris at Cardiff by 25–19. The New Zealanders were at the end of their short seven-match tour. They were nothing like as potent a unit as they had been cracked up to be, though in a forward, Scott Crighton, and a back, Steve Pokere, there were at least two who had given the watching British Lions' newly-elected management, Willie-John McBride and Jim Telfer, pause for thought.

There was not much evidence on the health of either Scotland's or England's national sides after the early winter tour by Fiji. Scotland overran the visitors by 32–12 in Edinburgh, and at Twickenham England went absolutely potty, scoring twelve tries and winning 60–19. It was Fiji's third tour of Britain – though the game had been in existence there for over a century. The resident British police garrison played a match there in 1880. In 1913 the Fijian Rugby Union was formed and now it is the island's chief winter sport with about 12,000 regular players in more than 600 clubs. They first came to Britain in 1964 – winning two matches in Wales – then again in 1970. They had promised so much in that second trip; not least they had triumphed over a strong Barbarians' XV at Gosforth with some spectacular running and sleight of hand. Next, in 1977, they had beaten the British Lions, who were on their homesick way back to Britain after a disastrous tour of New Zealand. Those last two results may have given the charming islanders the idea that exuberant off-the-cuffery was all that was necessary, but since then the world game had changed. It had become extremely well planned, not to say hard – not to say 'professional'. They looked very woebegone by the end of this 1983 trip.

So what was all the pre-Christmas fuss about? The answer was: boot money. Months before, in his retirement autobiography, the delightful, fast-striking, former England prop from Gloucestershire, Mike Burton, had written a humdrum ho-ho life story in which he had let loose the dreaded non-secret that some international players had been paid over the years for wearing a certain boot – usually either Adidas or Puma, two German firms owned respectively by two fallen-out, warring, Cain-and-Abel brothers. Burton had blown the gaff for a serialisation mess of greenbacks. Nothing happened for months then, suddenly, somebody re-read Burton – and all hell broke loose. Personally, I found the whole thing a bore. It worried me not, in the seventh round in Zaire, whether Muhammed Ali had done a deal with Coca Cola: there he was, in the ring alone and surely afraid, having to drum up some genius to dispose of the fiercesome Foreman. Who cared, holding his breath in that tie-break between Borg and McEnroe, how much they were getting from Slazenger, or Dunlop? When Coe and Ovett came round the last bend in Moscow's mile, did you ask who was wearing Adidas, who Puma? When Botham went for Lillee at Edgbaston or Headingley, who was examining the trademark on his bat? What manufacturer's symbol adorned Gareth Edwards's footwear when he plunged over for that classic try against Scotland in 1978, or some years earlier at the end of Bennett's Barbarians' extravaganza? Ah yes, I recall the footwear well . . .

The whole hoo-ha seemed meaningless, but the *Guardian* wanted me to conduct a full investigation. I telephoned Carwyn James for guidance and help. For once, Gwen said he was in. What do you reckon? I asked.

'Ah me,' he said, 'you too.' There was a sigh. 'For twenty-three days and nights boots and boot money have provided a dialogue worthy of *Coronation Street*, but hardly a word from on high has been whispered about the deplorably low standard of club rugby in England and Wales. Stick to that sort of stuff, boy.'

But surely, I said, all devil's advocate, this professional stuff could ruin the great game? 'Just pray, my boy,' said Carwyn, 'that perhaps one day the lawmakers on the International Board will reconsider the laws relating to professionalism. So then they can recover the skills of Edwards and Davies, Duckham and McLaughlan, and others lost to the game. The laws of Victoria seem strange in an era when Mammon, in the form of all sorts of sponsorship, rules.'

And that was that. We made plans to meet in Wales as soon as Christmas was over, and he promised to try to come to our *Guardian* sports-desk party in my flat in London on the first Saturday of the New Year.

Still in search of the great truth about boots, I went home to Gloucestershire to confront an old hero.

A generation still remembers him as the man who nearly scored The Try. The dying seconds of the University match of 1949 . . . Oxford desperately hanging on to their 3–0 lead in Twickenham's wintry twilight. Oxford clear their lines yet again, hacking southwards, deep into Cambridge territory. Those forwards with breath left flog themselves back for a last loose scrummage. Cambridge have it! One final dash for Dorward, their quicksilver scrum-half. No, he feints left and then reverse-passes right to his centre, J. V. Smith.

Carwyn James coaching at Llanelli in 1970. The little steel town's XV, under his guidance, became the most successful and celebrated club side in the world. 'He dealt with a rough bunch of blokes, but he never had to utter a harsh word, nor even raise his voice,' said one of his famous Lions of 1971, Ian McLauchlan.

The diminutive, muddied whippet dummies a pass to his winger, Gloag, then tears through the hole in the ragged dark blue hedge, pins his ears back and scuttles off for the right corner-flag, scarcely visible in the gloaming under the North Stand. Half the place dare not breathe, the other half shriek encouragement. An Oxford wing-forward dives valiantly at Smith's heels; he misses. The full-back can only hope against hope to drive him into touch, but at the precise moment, off his right foot, Smith goes inside him. He's through! But what's this? Where did he come from? From nowhere, all five (if you include the hyphen) of John MacGregor Kendall-Carpenter lands on Smith as he turns to make for the post to ensure Cambridge's winning conversion. Kendall-Carpenter engulfed the little whippet a couple of ruler-lengths from the line. It was presumed Kendall-Carpenter, a prop that day, had chased Smith from the scrum eighty yards back. In fact he had been a straggler from the original Oxford clearance. I remember the newspapers the next day. It was far too dark for photographs, but the art editors had drawn lots of squiggly lines and dots and arrows.

Seeing Things in Black and White

The tackle made Kendall-Carpenter's name – and, I suppose, Smith's too. Immediately he was picked for England on the right-wing and played four games that year – scoring a try a game. Smith is this season's new President of the Rugby Football Union. He runs his family business of corn and agricultural merchants scarcely a mile from his old school, Marling, in Gloucestershire. He lives high on the hills above Stroud, in a mellow Cotswold house with blissful sheep-cropped Minchinhampton Common spread all around him. He is dapper still, tidy and trim, with humour belying, I fancy, a JP sternness when necessary. I bet he can still run like the wind. By its nature the 'Buggins turn' of the RFU president is usually one of pomp and platitude for a single year. He is a speech-making figurehead, to exhort troops and spell out party lines. One year is not enough to change any fundamental policy – unless, perhaps, someone concentrates solely on a singular issue.

I had a hunch that Smith would have liked to concentrate on something else crucial to the world game, something far more relevant. But now he was having to get pompous about boots! 'We have got to hold on to the amateur principle,' he said, 'or else the whole thing falls apart.' He didn't think it was 'silly' that the England team were to be asked to black out the manufacturers' white motifs on their boots during the forthcoming international season. Why not just let the grass grow longer at Twickenham? I asked.

It was a crucial issue, said he. 'The game I would like to see in ten years' time would still be amateur, still with an amateur administration and still trying desperately hard to reduce the number of games leading players are having to turn out for each season. A game played for fun and pure enjoyment . . . and if you don't play it that way then get out of it. But if you ask me what I think it will be, I fear it will not be what I am describing. The great danger is the pressure of business salesmanship, as we have seen in the boots set-up. This pressure will increase all the time, creating fears and worries among the players, leaving them wondering what they can get out of it.'

To blazes with boots, I thought. Within a fortnight we won't hear of the issue again. Now to my hunch – no more than that, for Smith himself is too knowing a politician to reveal his ambitions outside 'cabinet' committees – that this new president's solo strike might just involve Rugby Union's attitude to South Africa. Over the years Rugby Union has paid a ridiculously dismissive lip-service to Gleneagles. I suppose that the Establishment banned the cricketers from playing for England in the very same week that Bill Beaumont, captain of the Lions in South Africa, received his OBE from the Queen, for the simple reason that India and West Indies have far more political muscle in cricket than the rugby-playing Fiji and Tonga. Somehow I sense that Smith – as he did at Twickenham those thirty-three years ago – would like to go single-minded for the line in an effort at least to open up a serious debate about whether England should tour South Africa, as planned, in twenty

Glorse force: Gloucestershire's happy end to their tenth final in thirteen seasons. Mike Rafter, cup in hand, is cheered by the former Stroud and England winger, J. V. Smith, (in dark suit) the well-tailored – and unsponsored! – president of the Rugby Football Union

months' time. The Establishment will doubtless corner-flag and stifle him, but it will be an interesting dash to observe. His presidency has come a year too early for crucial confrontation. On South Africa Smith has for many years, in various RU committees, been a minority voice – mostly of one. Two years after he stood as Stroud's parliamentary Liberal candidate, in 1966, Smith was opposing the Lions' tour to the Republic. When, in blinkered stubbornness, the RFU presumed it absolutely hunky-dory that the team should tour Southern Rhodesia after his namesake's declaration of UDI Smith spoke up again, horrified; indeed, years later when Mugabe's new Zimbabwe toured here for the first time Smith's Gloucestershire were quickest of all to welcome them.

At his inaugural speech in the summer, at the RFU AGM, Smith let everyone know what he was thinking. His words are worth repeating verbatim: 'If any other rugby-playing country feels we can provide services which would be to their advantage then we will be happy to consider their requests. In this context it is frequently pointed out that the South African connection is a deterrent to the game's development worldwide, and if that claim is valid then it should be examined. The RFU position is that we will play rugby against anyone, at any time, anywhere in the world, no matter what may be their country, colour, class or creed. At the same time I must report that in order to follow this through we have come regularly into conflict with Her Majesty's Government, both Conservative and Labour, on our South African connection, which of itself must be a cause for concern. It has always seemed illogical to me when those who argue that politics should be kept out of sport are always the first to take on the government of the day and resolutely oppose its wishes.

'I confess that mine is a minority view, but in the end, as political administrators, we have to ask ourselves the question, "Is it good for the game?" There is no simple answer. But I do ask that everyone gives deeper thought to what is a continuing problem, and one which will loom large in the public eye with the proposed tour of the South African Republic by an England team in the summer of 1984.'

Smith himself visited South Africa in the summer and, by all accounts, was as courteous as he was observant and outspoken in public print and on public platforms. He proceeds gently.

Meanwhile, the season awaits. 'Ah,' says J. V., 'there is always a feeling of expectancy and excitement before the start of a new season. You cannot control it. I know that cynics will pretend to laugh, for senior players like to think they are beyond such sentiment, but in their hearts they know it is true – the smell of embrocation, the hiss of the shower, the unmentionable sounds of the changing room, the first round of beer – they all get you in the end.' They indeed get you in the end – with as much nostalgic, certain decisiveness as a Kendall-Carpenter smother-tackle.

I went on across Offa's Dyke for my lunch with Carwyn.

Even those who have known Carwyn James a lifetime still admit they do not know *well* this gentle, introverted loner. I had long heard of him and the glorious romanticism of his coaching exploits with his little club at Llanelli who, for a decade or so now, had been eating giants for teatime most Saturday afternoons – including overgrown Wallabies and Kiwis too. Then; around 1977, Carwyn started his column on rugby for the *Guardian*, sometimes punchy and demanding, sometimes evocative and wistful, sometimes just a gentle meander through his fads and fancies.

In that British summer of 1977 the next Lions tour to New Zealand took place. On the eve of the first Test match at Wellington I travelled down to Wales to spend the night with Carwyn. We met in the BBC studios at Llandaff and I was greeted in the foyer and taken to Carwyn in the bar by none other than that scrum-half hero of my youth, Onllwyn Brace, whose original pranks that day at Twickenham in the Varsity match all those years ago had first so illuminated my affection for this game. While the night was still young Carwyn had first to tell the ravenous little scarlet nation his thoughts on the match, which would be starting, a million miles away, in the small hours, Welsh time. This new Lions team was managed by Carwyn's 1971 captain, John Dawes. It was captained by Phil

Bennett, one of Carwyn's favourite sons from Llanelli, and indeed one who followed in the same fly-half footsteps as both Carwyn himself and his first great protégé, Barry John. For this first Test match there were also in this Lions team eight other Welshmen.

We picked up an old telephone in the green room and put in a call to John Dawes. It was eight o'clock in the morning in Wellington. The hotel receptionist said firmly, 'No calls for the Lions.' 'He'll take one from me,' said Onllwyn. She put us through. We were John's alarm call. Blearily he accepted Brace's greetings. He said he was quietly confident. 'Good luck, boyo,' said Carwyn and hung up, to recall his own first Test as coach in 1971's triumphant march. He had not slept a wink. He had chain-smoked on his pillow, living the match to come, getting up every half-hour or so to sniff the weather . . .

From the Cardiff studios around midnight to Llanelli, then Stradey. Onllwyn driving for dear life, Carwyn alongside him, analysing all the pros and cons of possibility . . . Llanelli's clubroom was full of confidence and song. We sat on the platform in a friendly fug of anticipation and played Family Favourites with the team at their hotel, courtesy BBC Wales. We linked Phil up with his wife, Pat, down the road. It made a change from their everyday letters. The BBC plugged us into Willie-John McBride in Belfast and Sandy Carmichael in Edinburgh and Roger Uttley in Newcastle . . . The songs were touching, relevant. Phil chose for Pat a Rod Stewart, 'Sailing Home to You'. Many of the other records were tinged with homesickness, and I remember thinking, 'aye aye, what's this then? The First Test hasn't even been played.' Terry Cobner, the two Evanses and John Bevan all chose John Denver's most misty, yearning song; Brynmor went for 'Don't Cry for Me, Argentina', J. J. had Streisand – but Quinnell appropriately went for 'My Way', Graham Price for 'The Pontypool Front Row' and Dawes dedicated 'The Merry Widow' to his opera-singing wife, with (I hope) unpointed irony.

Up to the kick-off we drank merrily and played a confident 'Any Questions'. For there on the platform panel was the man who would surely have been captain had he not recently been so cruelly injured when he had failed to get up from a scrum – indeed he had been on the hospital danger list. From midnight to dawn, it seemed, Mervyn Davies sat with his head in his hands, dreaming of the might-have-been. On his right was Delme Thomas, incomparable Lion of old. On his left was Carwyn James, reliving his glories of 1971. Next to Carwyn was the legendary Ivor Jones, who was a Lion nearly fifty years ago. Next to Ivor was F. Keating, famed non-Lion. And next to me was the one and only Onllwyn Brace . . . Any questions?

'D'you think they'll do it, Onllwyn?'

'What would Phil be telling the boys in the dressing room, Merv?'

'What was your first Lions' tour like, Ivor?'

'D'you think the back-row's fast enough, Carwyn?'

' 'Oo the blazes is that guy, Keating?'

Then the match, the live transmission, courtesy BBC radio and its lyrical commentator, Alun Williams. For ten minutes we cheered every Lions' heel, every line-out won. Then we fell quiet. Then quieter. However much the commentary tried to jockey up our spirits, all Llanelli knew the boys were playing like drains.

At half-time Carwyn lit a cigarette and stood up – and took my breath away. The match was being played on the other side of the world; all he had to go on was a radio commentary crackling through the static. Yet here he was, analysing and suggesting, offering such thoughts as: 'the back-row are giving the All Blacks' scrum-half, Going, too much room,' or, 'Brynmor must link up more with Duggan,' or, 'Martin should move back to No. 5 in the line-out,' or, 'Fenwick must be faster to Robertson in the centre,' and 'I think Bennett might have injured himself when he tackled Going' . . . It was an amazing *tour de force*. The packed, smoke-fugged room accepted it all as the very gospel.

The second-half was played to stunned silence. Mervyn's head got lower in his hands, Onllwyn cursed under his breath, Carwyn smoked at least a dozen cigarettes . . . Finally, it was back to Carwyn's borrowed flat in Cardiff. He gave me his unmade bachelor's bed and insisted he would sleep on the sofa, which he did, still in his suit. I was woken by the telephone. Still lying down, still in his suit, Carwyn was dictating his analysis of the game to some broadcasting company. Throughout this early morning the phone continued to ring from all over Britain. We made some tea and then a friend with a car dashed him to the BBC for yet another interview, dropping me at the railway station. On the train I opened my *South Wales Echo*. The match was the front-page lead story. Across eight columns the banner headline read: LIONS LOSE – BUT CARWYN HOPEFUL.

Now, more than five years on, I travelled to Wales again and wondered what Carwyn would think of the prospects for this next tour by the British Lions to New Zealand. That, he said, was still six months off; there was half a club season and a whole international season to go. If I named you my thirty Lions now, he said, I would only do so accompanied by a bet that two-thirds of the names would be wrong. I told him I was still being urged to take an interest in the 'boots' business. 'Baloney!' he repeated. He was far more excited about the Australian rugby *league* touring team that had left Britain the previous month after setting alight the north of England in person and, through television, the rest of Europe. His love of sport knew no boundaries of codes or creeds: in high summers I often fancied he loved the romantic's cricket best of all; on Saturday teatimes, even at Llanelli's sanctum of Stradey, he would be eager to hear how Manchester United got on. Or Liverpool. Or Villa. Or Fulham. Or Wrexham. He once wrote: 'The transfer of skills from one ball game to another is something which should always occupy the mind of any responsible coach. That lesson was taught to me many winters ago by soccer's Dave Sexton.'

HELLO - SOME OF THE BOYS HAVE GONE FREE LANCE.

Not only that – and sacrilege to rugby union's exclusivity fogeys – he actually encouraged his British Lions to 'lower' the tone. 'In New Zealand, for instance, when I was putting right some phase of forward play I didn't mind in the least that Mike Gibson and Barry and Gareth and company played a game of soccer. In fact, Barry carried a soccer ball all over New Zealand. You see, any ball game is good for any sportsman. The main thing is that he is using a skill and, perhaps even more important when on a tour, he is being amused and doesn't get bored with all the training that's necessary. That's another thing: a coach must see to it that his team's training sessions are varied. There's nothing like a contented player.

'In New Zealand we played a lot of indoor cricket and basketball . . . anything which needed skill. I would like to emphasise the word "skill" because some people who are anti-coaching claim that all it does is to teach forwards to get stuck in and so on. The Lions proved in New Zealand that there is no substitute for a high degree of skill.'

And on he went, though this time he was happy to be brought back to the thrilling skills of the Australian rugby leaguers. They had, he said, restored the art of 'collision rugby allied to phenomenal support play'. There was many a lesson for senior players to learn from their athleticism, teamwork, backing-up qualities, handling – and especially their fitness.

What about this year's international championship, I asked – 'that's why I'm buying you a gin-and-tonic lunch!' He thought England might have a good year – 'if they can hang on to what seems to be a new-found,

Lifting the spirits . . . the French line prepares at Windsor. Even Rives suggested it would be 'difficult' for an Englishman to attend. The pocket Napoleon and coach, Fouroux, (ABOVE, at right) suspects that strangers are spies – though he leaves all interpreting to his English-speaking captain.

hitherto long-lost pride in themselves.' Scotland, too, had all the makings after their flamboyant finish last season – 'but again they must retain faith in themselves.' France will be ominously good 'if their selectors don't go daft.' Ireland had to decide whether to keep their ageing Triple Crown warriors or go for a brand new team. And Wales? 'Well, an introverted nation used to winning turns on itself when the winning stops. Fundamental questions long forgotten are remembered, skeletons are recovered from locked cupboards, scapegoats have to be found, committees are formed and even more sub-committees. In such a climate who would want to be a national selector or a national coach?'

If performances at international level only faintly mirrored club rugby, Wales, odds-on favourites, would win the Triple Crown and the Championship in a canter. Despite the deep depression at national level club rugby in Wales is still strong, and the quality played by most so far this season had been pleasing. In a radius of a few miles it is always possible to pick a tough contest and chances are that someone will sparkle. Just to glance at the records of the dozen top Welsh clubs against English opposition, forty-four games have been won and, of the sixteen lost, there were three losses each to Pontypridd and Aberavon and four to Newport, which leaves only a sprinkling of defeats.

Of even greater significance, therefore, was the record of the top eight against English clubs. Thirty-four matches were won, four lost and two drawn, which makes it an eighty-five per cent success rate – a pretty convincing argument in favour of the comparative strength of Welsh club rugby. With such talented club sides in the principality it was difficult to understand the reason for the national depression. In a five-nations championship of no favourites it is just possible that one team may be slightly more equal than the others. On balance, he thought, Wales could do it, 'if we get our psyche in order'.

We would see. And we arranged to meet again in my flat in London on the night of the *Guardian*'s New Year party – a week before the Championship kicked off at Twickenham and Murrayfield.

CHAPTER FOUR

A Hotel in Amsterdam

Carwyn, as it happened, never did turn up to the party on the first Saturday of the New Year. Typical! His gypsy, sometimes scatty, social nature was much part both of his innocence and his charm. By all accounts, though, the 'do' was considered a success. It went on long enough – and certainly it was blearily uncomfortable to be up early for the drive to Marlow, blinking through the glitter of a grand, bright-white winter's morning. The fresh sun mocked my hangover, but once I was out of the car the slap of an icy breeze wakened and exhilarated as it whipped down through the Chilterns and skidded off the Thames.

The England squad were practising at Bisham Abbey, a stately pre-Reformation foundation in soft, pink Home Counties brick that has been handsomely converted into a sports centre by the Central Council for Physical Recreation. The England players looked happy and relaxed. There was much hearty laughter, as well as earnest, narrow-eyed endeavour as they went through their routines – old ones, new ones, loved ones, neglected ones – and got to know each other again.

The captain and his coach looked at ease. Steve Smith, a cheery bundle of muscle, and Mike Davis, an open-faced, healthy West Country schoolmaster, also looked very much in charge. The chairman of the selectors, Budge Rogers, looked on, bristling keen. His committee, one fancied, were not going to have much deliberating to do this season – in the trial match three weeks before this senior side had routed The Rest 47–7, to pass 200 points in four successive matches with ease, though admittedly against such teams as Canada, America and Fiji. Not the sort of opposition about which to send postcards home, perhaps, but still, points on the board . . . and, to be sure, this Sunday morning the team looked confident indeed. England would start on Saturday as favourites of the four Home nations; and it may be that their opening match against France at Twickenham next week would prove to be the actual Championship decider . . .

But I did have one tiny, jingoistic niggle : for to me it's always been a slightly diluted England team when there's been no West Country club

The front-row union, English chapel: Pearce, Wheeler and Smart. Says Wheeler: 'Some like to perpetuate the secret society, freemasonry of it; yet the fact remains that it is a very complex area and all to do with weight, balance and leverage. Up and down, round this way and that, forward and back . . .'

represented – and, I might add, a less successful one. I acknowledged that rumbustious, moustachioed bullock of a No. 8, John Scott, would be one of England's cornerstones this season, and he was born in Exeter, but John now plays his club rugby for Cardiff. Indeed, he is captain – a double blasphemy! England should have had a Gloucestershire man at the very front of the trench war, but a month or so ago our Cheltenham fruit n' veg merchant, Phil Blakeway, suddenly and without public warning downed tools and said 'enough is enough'.

Phil, the captain of Gloucestershire, was a mighty man and one of the strongest scrummaging props in the world. He would not be pushed around. When he played for The Rest in the final trial before the 1980 international season he so out-wrenched and out-manoeuvred the senior scrum that he was at once promoted and was later seen to be the final piece in the jigsaw that resulted in England winning their Grand Slam that year. Since when he has been wretchedly unlucky with injuries, as well as remarkably brave. A few years ago, after a club game with Gloucester, he spent the following week rubbing his back. He thought he had cricked his neck. The following Saturday he played a county game against Cornwall at Camborne – inevitably the sternest of neighbourly fixtures. Phil played a blinder and scored a try. On the Monday morning his neck was still cricked. 'I asked the wife to drive me to "the vets" for a check-up.' She did. He had broken his back. He was in plaster for eighteen months. He also played two of those Grand Slam internationals with broken ribs. Gloucester forwards are something special.

A week or two before Christmas this previously uncomplaining thirty-one-year-old had, seemingly on the spur of the moment, telephoned Mike Davis to break his news, and also returned the postcard asking him if he was available to tour again with the British Lions in the summer. My immediate feeling was simply of surprise that more international players didn't jack it in more often. They are amateurs, 'fun' sportsmen, they nearly all have a weekday job and turn out on Saturday for alleged relaxation; the hassles, both mental and physical, sometimes seem scarcely worth it.

Said Phil: 'I'm just getting fed up with the bump and grind of the rugby field – it's as simple as that. I have realised for some months now that my interest in playing is nowhere near as strong as it used to be. Physically I am finding the game too wearing. Rugby demands such commitment these days, so I have decided to finish while still in one piece. I have decided to call it a day while at the top, and now intend to give more time to my family and business.' He will be missed. How much? We will know by March.

Whenever Phil was doing the business for England my overgrown schoolboy's mind was warmed, for I liked to feel he was playing a bit for Roy Fowke, one of the heroes of my boyhood. Roy was another squat, four-square giant. He, like Phil, was a prop, and played for Stroud in my day; he should have turned out for England many a time, but the side in those 1950s seemed made up exclusively of chaps from Oxbridge or officers from the Combined Services. Or that's what we thought.

Roy was a bargee on the Sharpness Canal. One time he did get an England trial. For The Rest, of course, but like Blakeway was to do twenty years later he devastated the opposition to such extent that, in conclave in the bar later that evening, the selectors decided they were bound to include him in the side for the first international. The chairman took a deep breath, sighed, flicked a raindrop of Martini from his squadron leader's moustache and called 'Our Fowker' into the conversation. Well, they had to see he was the right type, didn't they? There was at that time being aired the first mutterings of tactical considerations about forward play, new-fangled intellectualism about rucks, and mauls, and leverage, and weight distribution in the scrum. Roy, his giant mitt curled round a pint mug, did as he was bid. The chairman spoke: 'Tell me, Royston – jolly well played today, incidentally – what are your particular tactics when one of these loose rucks is formed at the breakdown point in three-quarter play?'

Roy pondered. He stroked his jowl with one hairy hand and took a long, gulping swig with the other. His England cap rested on his reply. It was very much time to speak. 'Well, sirs,' he said, ' 'tis like this. If one of them buggers in the backs drops the thing and I be the first to get there, well, then I picks it off the ground, puts it under me arm and charges up the pitch like mad. Now if I've been held up on the way and am late to the assembly, as sometimes can happen, well, I s'pose I just gets there the very fastest I can manage and once there I drives me bloody boot in!'

Ahem, quite so . . . Roy Fowke never did play for England. The absolute decision was taken later that very evening, by all accounts, when our local hero engaged in intimate and pally conversation with one of the selection panel, a former Oxford blue, a Harlequins' Hooray Henry, a one-match England player, and now one of the country's leading barristers.

FOWKER: What be y'doin' furra livin' then?
QUIN: Actually, I'm working at the Bar.
FOWKER: Which one?
QUIN: Lincoln's Inn, actually.
FOWKER: What be 'ee there then? Potman, is it?

In truth, however, the long-time provincial moan that the snooty London clubs were the ones to play for if any Englishman wanted to win an international cap had ceased to be the case for many years. The England team to meet France, in fact, had no representatives from any metropolitan sides. Four were from the North (Smith, Carleton, Bainbridge and Winterbottom), seven from the Midlands (Hare, Davies, Dodge, Cusworth, Wheeler, Pearce and Jeavons), three – would you believe? – from Wales (Scott, Swift and Smart) and one, Colclough, from the French side, Angôuleme.

By the by, this very week a friend of mine, a geographer at Keele University, John Bale, sent me a copy of his researches into rugger's people and places. The 2,054 rugby clubs in Britain, he says, represent just one club per 26,440 of the population. Of the regional stereotypes, not surprisingly the South Wales counties provide five out of the top seven counties: mid-Wales and that hotbed of the 15-a-side game, the Scottish Border county, make up the other leading cluster. Those South Wales counties possess very high *per capita* indices. Dyfed, for instance – and its passionate involvement in the Carwyn country around Llanelli – has over six-and-a-half times the number of rugby clubs per head of the population than the country as a whole. Gwent has an index of 5.90 and the

Captain Smith at the helm. 'Now I realise the job is to do not with hype, but with calm.' Smith's qualities as a leader were to be publicly revealed as the season progressed when his players backed him in an unprecedented series of outbursts against the selectors.

Glamorgans and Powys are also heavily involved. In England, far and away the main focus is in the South West – Cornwall, Gloucester, Avon and Devon – and John's figures totally disprove the long-held image of London and its suburbs giving shelter to a great guffawing hive of rugger buggers. Writes Bale:

'Only a small number of the Home Counties possess *per capita* indices above the national norm. This is surprising, since the region was the traditional focus of amateur rugby. Surrey (1.38) is the major county in the south-east, but there is no suggestion of a suburban rugby ring around the metropolis. In the West Midlands only Warwickshire (1.47) goes any way towards suggesting any degree of localisation of the sport in the suburban counties. Indeed, some of the outer metropolitan areas (Hampshire, Berkshire and Suffolk) have very low indices. The most dramatic under-emphasis on rugby is found in the north of England and in a semi-circle around the Midlands stretching from Merseyside, through East Anglia to Greater London and thence to Dorset. With the exception of Cumbria, no English county north of a line joining the Mersey and the Wash has an index of more than 1.00. Of the metropolitan counties, only Cleveland has an index of more than 0.70.'

It is not often that it happens, but always nice when scholars put their mind to sport. John Bale's studies involved thirty-five counties. His top-and-bottom ten make an interesting league table:

County	Index	One Club per	Number of Clubs
Dyfed	6.67	3,964	82
Border	6.58	4,019	25
Gwent	5.90	4,482	98
West Glamorgan	4.82	5,486	67
South Glamorgan	4.80	5,509	70
Powys	3.51	7,534	14
Mid-Glamorgan	3.33	7,941	68
Cornwall	2.94	8,994	46
Gloucestershire	2.74	9,651	51
Islands	1.94	13,640	5
Merseyside	0.61	43,349	36
Staffordshire	0.61	43,349	23
Hampshire	0.62	42,650	34
Humberside	0.62	42,650	20
West Midlands	0.62	42,650	65
Berkshire	0.63	41,973	16
Dorset	0.63	41,973	14
Suffolk	0.63	41,973	14
Greater London	0.67	39,467	178
Lancashire	0.68	38,887	35

If 'Glorse' were just pipped from being proved the 'senior' English county it didn't matter much to me, for my second favourite rugby stronghold has always been Cornwall. A couple of years back I had occasion to spend a lot of time in Cornwall and was able to see a fair deal of their rugby. More than once I stood at 'Hellfire Corner' in Redruth where the ground slopes down to the corner-flag and all the Duchy wills their boys down to bring home the bacon in the final minutes. I never saw Cornwall's most legendary forward, the coalman Bonzo Johns – they said he would finish his pony-and-cart delivery service round the town with just an hour to kick-off, grab a pasty on the way to the ground for his lunch, tie up his nag at the railings and, without bothering to wipe the coaldust from his face or forearms, create mayhem and fear in every visiting front row trio. He would prefer the visits of Surrey or Middlesex. Like Our Fowker at Gloucester, Bonzo was criminally ignored by the England selectors; but his successor as the patron-prop of his people was Stack Stevens, and he won twenty-five international caps between 1969 and 1975. A couple of autumns ago I went to see Stack, now in his late thirties, but still turning out occasionally for the 'Pirates' of Penzance. He farmed with his Dad, up in the hills of Godolphin, above St Michael's Mount. Like Bonzo, he too lived on pasties – though his sister came up and cooked Sunday lunch at the farm.

As I watched this current England team, tailored tracksuits and all, practising this New Year Sunday morning, my mind drifted back fondly to my interview with Stack.

'No, I don't train as such,' he'd told me. 'I just like to play matches to keep fit, for anyone and anywhere. I get those postcards "you have been chosen to play against So-and-so and are you available? RSVP" from secretaries – yes, even from England. But I never ever send them back. It's an understood thing with everyone that I never reply. They know I'm always available if I *don't* answer them.

'Beer does me good. I've tried giving it up for fitness purposes and sometimes I've tried drinking more. Either way it makes no difference to my game. I'm the only man I reckon who trains with England in jeans – never had time for them fancy tracksuits. I suppose I don't suffer from cold legs like some I could mention.'

Once, I remember, Joe McPartlin, the former Scottish international, was proposing a toast at a club dinner in Lewes to his friend and fellow Oxford blue, Nick Silk, who had won four England caps in the middle sixties – 'and each one, progressively, of a larger size!' You could never say that of Stack Stevens. That massive worthy could not even tell you how many caps he's won, can't even tell you when he last played for England, or for the Lions.

Again, in the early 1970s, I remember reading with disbelief a newspaper filler paragraph which said 'STACK STEVENS TO JOIN HARLEQUINS'. It seemed a social sacrilege. Rosslyn Park, perhaps, or Streatham/Croydon; but Harlequins, the very nobbiest of them all? It seemed impossible, but it happened, and for some time the West Country took a different view of their hero. When I met him, having returned long to the green grasses of Godolphin, Stack explained: 'I never thought of leaving Penzance in the first place, but in that postal strike some years back we never got any money sent for the produce we sent up each day to the London markets on the train, so I had to go up to collect the lolly each week. Quins heard about it and asked me to play for them. So at least they paid me my expenses.' He chortled when I told him that to unknowing us at the time it had seemed like Benn bedding Thatcher. Well, almost.

Although no Cornishman (and, indeed, no Harlequin) was in the England side at Bisham two Gloucestershire forwards, Mills and Hesford, would be on the substitutes' bench against France, along with the backs Rose, Bond and Melville and the prop Rendall. Then, at the end of the training session, we learned that the prancing, upright centre, Woodward, had pulled out. He had stood up to some strong tackling in practice, but decided in the end that an injured shoulder might not last out in match conditions – especially, say, against a rampaging Blanco at Twickenham. 'There was,' said coach Davis, 'a time when England men thought they could hide themselves on the field but Woodward's pride would not allow him to take a chance. He just needs more games to improve his confidence.' Woodward's place would be taken by Huw Davies, who was certainly a fine tackler; he had been dropped last season after eight matches as fly-half.

The players went off to shower, lunch and drive home. It looked a happy team; and a confident one. It was experienced enough. Dusty Hare, the Newark farmer at full-back, had first played for England in 1974; he was once a Nottinghamshire cricketer and had been captained by Sir Garry Sobers. As a place-kicker alone, the dreamy calm of Dusty was making him threaten the record books as that prodigious knight had done at cricket. England's senior back was Johnny Carleton, the right wing, a schoolteacher who gave up his job when his local Lancashire education authority refused to give him time off to tour South Africa in 1980. On the left wing, the accomplished Mike Slemen had been dropped after being an unquestioned fixture for twenty-nine matches, and the eponymous Swift, a Lancastrian accountant who played for Swansea, won the vote over the Bath flyer, David Trick. Both Swift and Trick were natural right-wingers, and it would be interesting to see if Slemen's unaccountable omission would make a difference to England's Championship pretensions. In the centre, partnering the recalled Davies – who had dual 'nationality' and had chosen to be selected for England even though his father and grandfather had both played fly-half for Tredegar – was the uncompromising, unfrilly Paul Dodge. Woodward's injury had broken up the Leicester Connection in midfield – Hare and Dodge also played for the 'Tigers', as did the fly-half, Les Cusworth, a balding, delicate, scheming player. At scrum-half was the captain, Smith.

Each line of the forwards had a resolute champion: the hooker, Peter

Wheeler, an insurance broker and another Leicester player, was generally considered the very best all-rounder in his position in the world. In the second row was Maurice Colclough, truly a giant, respected round the world both physically and socially; he ran a seaside holiday complex in France. And in the middle of the back, chief marauder and No. 8 was John Scott.

Wheeler was flanked by Blakeway's successor, Gary Pearce, who was educated just up the road from Bisham, at Aylesbury, and by Colin Smart, another Englishman abroad – he plays for Newport. Smart is an immensely strong player and an engaging man with a roly-poly beer pot who is best remembered by the public as the drinker of aftershave lotion at a banquet in Paris last year. Alongside Colclough in the second row is the long-limbed 6ft 7in rookie, Steve Bainbridge, a Geordie teacher who stepped into the breach last year when England's captain and national folk hero, Bill Beaumont, retired after taking one blow on the head too many. At the back, Scott was flanked by the two flying pin-up boys – the leggy Yorkshire farmer, Winterbottom, with the hayrick hair and the 'buzz' of a worker bee, and Nick Jeavons, more sultry and swarthy about his dash; in an article last year the writer Jilly Cooper swooningly referred to Jeavons as 'the body'.

As I waited for Steve Smith to change and come for lunch in the old refectory at Bisham I came across a letter in the previous week's *Times*, from Mr Grenville Jones of, appropriately, Twickenham: 'Sir, the English rugby team includes gentlemen named Hare, Dodge, Swift, Smart and Wheeler, with a Mr Trick waiting in the wings. How can mere mortal Celts hope to cope with players possessed of such fleetness of foot and cunningness of character? . . .'

Given a successful season, the captain of this favoured band had it in him to become as much a national figure as his admired predecessor. If the nation saw Bill Beaumont as honest and warm, unshirking and brave and bear-like, they would see in Smith the most engaging smile in big-time sport. Away in Australia during the winter the television cameras had been closing in nightly on England's cricket captain, Bob Willis, a charming man but, in close-up, a brooding worrier. Not Steve Smith. He is all perky awareness, a bustling busybody at the heels of his pack; darting eyes and feet as he snaffles and tidies, observes and encourages, rabbiting all the while as he calls for more creativity, more commitment, more caution.

Actually, talking of Bob Willis, it is not beyond the bounds of reason to reckon that Steve Smith might even have been England's cricket captain in Australia this winter. He has a passion for that game too. Ten years ago he was going in first wicket down for Loughborough Colleges' most famous cricket team: batting order – A. Borrington (Derbyshire), J. Tolchard (Leics), S. S. A. Hampshire (Jack's brother), G. Barlow (Middlesex) . . . In the summer of 1972 Smith was in the runs and there were regular rumours about a trial with Gloucestershire. Then the England

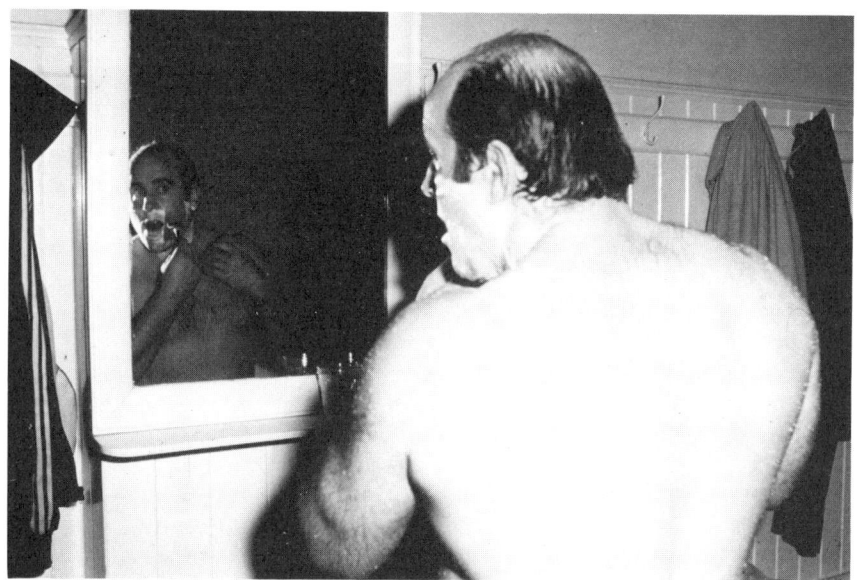

TOP The mighty Smart spruces up for the after-match ball. An England colleague reckons Smart the strongest man he has known. These shoulders are the foundations of his scrum's shove: the paunch he puts down, not to beer, but to 'necessary ballast'. BOTTOM In the tiled dungeon under the Royal Box at Twickenham, England's 6ft 6in Bainbridge sees the humour about sharing an Edwardian bathtub.

rugby side called him to join the tour to South Africa, since when it has been rugby tours most summers, and club cricket for Brookwood in the Lancashire and Cheshire League has had to suffice.

'I haven't had a real "holiday-type holiday" since 1971: Greece with three mates, the old rucksack on the back. Those were the days! Penniless, queuing on the steps of the old blood donor's bank, wine two bob a bottle; give a litre of blood and you could get smashed for three weeks.' The memory of it ignites again the magnificent melon smile.

Persistence has made him England's most capped scrum-half in history. Through the Lilywhites' dank and dotty days of the last decade – in forty-one matches between 1970 and 1977 England chose twenty-one different half-backs – Smith, from 1972, alternated on the scrum-half carousel with Webster, Page, Kingston, Lampkowski and Young, till he made the position his own sixteen matches ago when the selectors determined on a more consistent policy. In last season's enterprising win over Wales he overtook Dick Jeeps's scrum-half record of twenty-five. That milestone pleased him especially. In England's doldrum years it was always reckoned that Jeeps himself, then an eminence in the selectors' panelled committee room, had little time for the extrovert Smith, who always thought Jeeps fancied he couldn't play. No wonder last year's historic record gave such pleasure.

Those seasons when Smith was going in and out more often than an Oxbridge stroke from Putney to Mortlake were harrowing times; even when called to the colours. 'You almost wanted to hide away. Of course I wanted to play for my country, but I needed to win. When I dropped out of the squad in 1978 I got the impression they would have chosen my mum before me. Not even getting a reserve card tells you how far "out" you are – remember, the selectors pick four sides! Once I was actually told by a selector that I was a disruptive influence on the team. Yet I've always been independent and enjoyed life. You can't always exist on your instincts, and younger players need to be told this. In those days I wasn't worried about training or aware of the weight problems that were to arrive later.' And sometimes when he was dropped he admits he might not have been quite fit enough. He puts on weight easily. He has to train harder than most – every evening when he gets home from his job as a marketing manager for a sports clothing firm. 'I'm a poor man's Lester Piggott. The knack is to weigh in every day. I can put on four or five pounds just like that: a couple of nights on the piss and it's all got to come off again. The hardest part of training is putting on your tracksuit. Luckily I've no wife to greet me from work by plonking down a whacking great tea in front of the fire and switching on *Nationwide*.'

'Lucky, then, that you don't fancy the lovely Sue Lawley.'

'You too? I think about her all the time I'm out there running, don't I?'

That grin again. Not that he has ever been greased lightning. 'Lack of speed was always my weakness. But now it doesn't seem to matter much. I think I compensate now I'm older by being able to stand back and read the game better, consider all the options. Suddenly it's not all instinct, it's observation and know-how.'

The captaincy of England came, of a sudden, when Beaumont retired. Over the years Smith had been given a good schooling. His first international captain was John Pullin – 'big JV, strong and silent; we forwards are going to get the ball for you, then it's up to you.' Then Fran Cotton, friend and Sale clubmate – 'he could have been the most complete captain of all; a great motivator, but very tactically aware. People think "great big thick props", yet it's an art and a science as well as strength. But he was hard, was Frannie. I was best man at his wedding but he still managed to inflict' – he pulls up a trouser leg – 'these seventeen stitches when he trod on me in a Lancs v Cheshire game. Not on purpose, mind.'

Suddenly you realise how the red rose has served English captaincy so well, for next came Tony Neary – 'smashing bloke, but a loner, never a rant or a rave. He'd just do his own thing and you'd want to follow.' Same with Roger Uttley – 'big man with the soft voice and that great big, lovely, ugly face: and what strength! You could see the muscles in his eyelashes.' Then Beaumont – 'the big cuddly bear who became, quite simply, a very great captain. Everyone loved him. At first he wouldn't say boo to a goose, but in the end old Bill became a bit of a tub-thumper.' Then came Beaumont's injury, followed a match later by his permanent retirement.

'When Billy was feeling ill before the Scotland game he told me that I'd take over should he fail to make it. I said, "That's wrong – it should be 'Wheelbrace' (Peter Wheeler)." But Bill said, "No, you're wrong – it should be you." As it happened, Bill was okay, but after his bang on the head against the North Midlands in the county final the situation arose for real. Although I appreciated the honour, I needed some persuading before accepting. "Brace" and I go back a long way; we played together for England Under 25s at the start of the seventies against Fiji. He's got thirty caps and been on two Lions' tours. I've great respect for him as a player – and as a bloke. The press obviously felt the same way as I did about the fact he should have been skipper, but one of the greatest things was Pete's reaction – he came up and told me he was right behind me. I said, "Brace, you were the least of my problems." I knew that.'

Smith chuckles as he admits to the bog he made of his first dressing-room exhortation as captain – against Ireland last year. 'Even a drama critic guy like you wouldn't have believed it. My eyes blazed passion, my fists were hammering the table, I was completely gone, I was ranting on about history and our English heritage and all that; Crécy, Agincourt, Dunkirk, even the IRA got a mention! So what happens? We all ran out and played the hurly-burly like bloody headless chickens, didn't we? We were awful. It was all my fault. And I deserved all the stick I got, too.'

By the time France were ready to be well beaten in Paris a fortnight later Smith had got his act together. 'I realised the job was not to hype up the team but to calm them all down. You must realise that international matches are so manic and pressurised that, for us players, they seem nearly over before they've begun. Everything goes at a thousand miles an hour, and my job is to cool it, to get the guys to stay calm and aware and keep concentrating on what we've planned and worked out in training sessions.' So he wouldn't be reminding his men of Hastings or the Falklands soon after lunch on Saturday? 'No, I will not. The IRA indeed!' and he laughs fit to bust at the memory of his first speech. 'What you must understand is that in that little room at twenty past two there are fifteen glazed-eyed, quivering lads with involuntary muscles in their backsides going at a rate of knots. We're used to playing in front of 500, not 70,000. Tony [Swift, the new England cap] won't know what's hit him when he runs out. Then it'll all go so fast. I'll tell him what I told Tony Bond when he got his first cap: "keep your eye on that clock; it'll go round so fast that you won't remember a thing, but when there's ten minutes to go just pick up that ball and charge like hell. Anyway, you won't know how you've played till you read John Reason next day in the *Sunday Telegraph* – and then it's bound to have been badly!"'

Smith sees the scrum-half as simply the fourth man in the back row. Offensive and defensive. He anticipates a battle royal on Saturday afternoon. 'Whenever anyone asks me who my most difficult marker has been I just say "the French pack of 1976".' England were beaten 30–9. 'It could have been double that. We were annihilated. Frannie had terrible troubles against that giant, Paparemborde, who has these sloping shoulders so there's nothing to scrummage against. At the sing-song after the match poor Frannie was so upset he refused to join in. "I'm not man enough to sing with those Frenchies," he said. Four years later in Paris, at every scrum, Frannie packed down with his head spearing into Paparemborde's breastbone. It was an astonishing feat of strength and technique. We destroyed them.' At the final whistle Smith embraced Cotton and whispered: 'We can drink with the men tonight, Fran.'

Together they fashioned two of the most glorious hangovers since the night they invented champagne. By the way, one of Smith's little jobs this week was to give England's current prop, Colin Smart, Cotton's phone number – 'for a bit of revision on Paparemborde's breastbone!'

Smith's advice was to 'watch the first three scrums on Saturday: they could even decide the whole Championship. The front row battle will hold the key. The French could have the best front three in the world; if we match them for the first twenty minutes we should be okay. Mind you, six of their seven backs can do the one hundred metres in eleven seconds – which is about ten minutes faster than me.' But then, he says, he looked around his dressing-room and thought, 'Hey, we've got a fair old team too. What the key men do affects all us others. Old Dusty at the back, all doze and dreamy; Swifty and JC on the wings, all nerve ends and 100 mph; Les at stand-off, who hates losing and will always pull out something with his Yorkshire cunning; Scottie the hard man, the complex one, extrovert and insecure at one and the same time, but what a great player; Maurice, knowing he's now in Billy's shirt with all that entails; and Peter

Wheeler – well, what can you say? He's the world's No. 1, but still just gets better and better, like good wine.'

They'll do for him. Not bad for that little long-ago Stretford Ender who was passionate about Man. United as well as cricket, till he got his 11-plus and went to grammar school where they did this rugby lark. He's still dedicated to United, but doesn't go much now. Well, when it's not rugger or running there's squash at the Sale clubhouse. Soon he'd like to immerse himself in water sports – sailing and surfing and so on. Meanwhile, England's loss of the Ashes in Australia the previous week niggles away at England's rugby union captain. He stayed up, of course, to watch the last rites on TV. 'Hey, and do you know that Tavare? Well, next time you see him, ask him how he can possibly expect to get the ball off the square when his hands are so far apart on the handle. It's a blithering impossibility. I'm telling you.' And he gets up to play a sweet and imaginary cover-drive, simulating the sound of leather on willow with a satisfying click of his tongue. And this charming young sportsman holds the pose in his follow-through – and a great big grin of pleasure lights up his face.

In 1980 Smith was called out to South Africa as a substitute for the British Lions in their very last match. He was not called on to play, but was awarded the coveted kit. He has taken the badge off the blazer and has never dared wear the tie. He was, however, officially a Lion for four days. In his fascinating book on that tour, Carwyn James ended with some pen portraits of the players. The very last note in the book reads: 'Steve Smith is a very likeable lad from Sale who managed to cram more into his weekend excursion to South Africa than some of his colleagues did in ten weeks.'

Early the next evening I was having a bath. The six o'clock BBC TV news was droning on down the corridor. Suddenly I was standing in the sitting room, dripping and unbelieving. Carwyn James was dead. He had suffered a heart attack in his bath at a hotel in Amsterdam the night before – the evening the *Guardian* had hoped to see him in this very flat at their party. Apparently he had gone to Amsterdam a few days before to relax after finishing his coaching series for BBC Wales. The newsreader said he was fifty-three. No, I still couldn't believe it. I rang the *Guardian* office. They confirmed the story and said that already the obituaries were flooding in – many from his former pupils, stricken at their loss.

John Dawes, captain of Carwyn's 1971 Lions and now Wales's coaching organiser: 'Carwyn is simply irreplaceable. His achievements are second to none. He was totally involved in the game, and he gave so much. I never knew anyone who gave as much as he did. He was unique in that he understood players – whatever their tribulations – and he was always prepared to listen.'

Gerald Davies, winger supreme and one of Carwyn's own personal joys: 'His, a scholar's mind, was academic in its precision, though not dryly so. He had a passion for Welsh poetry and literature generally and in his writing brought a poet's sensitive mind to bear on a rugged and boisterous game. In a county with an appetite, apparently insatiable, for wanting to talk and listen to more about rugby football, people were always moved, after everybody else had had their say, to wonder expectantly what he, Carwyn, had to say. In Wales, which often appears as a village of inter-family relations, there is simply no need for a surname.

'The Lions of 1971 are remembered as much for the talent of the separate players as for the corporate effort that brought success. A miner's son in socialist west Wales, he subscribed fully to the idea of excellence and, unlike other more vociferous egalitarians, he believed passionately, where talent was concerned, in the existence of an elite. Each player, each set of new circumstances, would receive his thoughtful and careful response, even at the risk of offending the sensibilities of others. Once you knew his sense of quiet conviction, though, there was no such risk at all. Soon Wales will begin their championship campaign. But, come what may, it will not be the same this year nor, to many people in Wales, is it ever likely to be so again.'

Ian McLauchlan, 1971 Lions' prop forward and Carwyn's 'Mighty Mouse': 'I shall always remember his gentleness. He thought a great deal about rugby and about life. In New Zealand he was dealing with a fairly rough bunch of blokes, but he never had to utter a harsh word and never had to raise his voice. Our success was entirely due to him.'

His contemporaries weighed in tearfully, those who had played the game with him when, in the week, he was a teacher at Carmarthen and Llandovery and on Saturdays the player who would blossom and bewitch in the scarlet of Llanelli . . . Cliff Morgan, Wales and Lions stand-off, who kept Carwyn out of the Welsh team for so long: 'He was a beautifully balanced player, like Barry John. He could kick with either foot and he could sidestep. We will never see his like again.'

That boyhood hero of mine, Onllwyn Brace, who was Carwyn's inside-half at Stradey: 'In style, intent and outlook we were kindred spirits: neither of us was really physically well equipped to meet the rigours of Welsh first-class football, and weighing in at under ten stone neither of us was enamoured of the close attention given to errant halves in those days. As a result our approach was mutually enlightened, to say the least – the essence was enjoyment, the execution carefree; only the careworn faces of the Llanelli pack were a deterrent to our nomadic delights, but with an enchanting indifference he in particular invariably went his own way, because he was always his own man. The sadness that we feel at his passing is shared by Italians, Spaniards, Rumanians, Argentines, Japanese, New Zealanders, South Africans and Australians alike – the common language was rugby. Though that was his first love, I have a sneaking feeling that he might have preferred sometimes to have made his sporting mark either on the green baize like his compatriot Terry

Griffiths or on the cricket wickets of St Helens and Sophia Gardens. But rugby would have been the poorer.'

His fellows and his friends from his new craft of journalism . . . Clem Thomas, who had also been his captain when they played together first for the Welsh Secondary Schools' XV thirty-seven years ago: 'I often felt it was a mistake when he forsook the academic life to join the hurly-burly of the sports media. Sometimes I felt that it was a form of revenge at the neglect of his talent by Welsh rugby. He adored Neville Cardus and he took great pride in working for the *Guardian*. So often did he agonise to me over his Friday piece for the paper. We will all miss him dearly and he will always remain one of the great legends of rugby football.'

On journalists' trips abroad, Clem and John Reason, of the *Daily Telegraph*, were Carwyn's 'minders': they 'arranged' their dear friend's disorder. In a powerful and touching tribute in his newspaper, Reason ended: 'Carwyn Rees James was one of the most gifted boys ever to attend Gwendraeth Grammar School. Every page he opened in life seemed to have something on it which he could relish and illuminate and he reached for them eagerly: the love of language, of learning, of singing, of drama, of history, of cricket, of rugby football, of people, of life itself. Sadly, the further he read through that book the less it lived up to the bright, glad, confident morning of promise it offered him as a schoolboy. He remained a rather lonely, very private person, behind an exterior which had so many brilliant facets. In the end he was cut down, just as those young boys in white were cut down in the cornfield by the machine guns in *Dr Zhivago*, and we are left to grieve about what might have been, with the same ineffable feeling of sadness.'

And indeed, the more one heard details from the dead man's *real*, long-time friends, the more one realised that, in death, there was for this much loved man some relief as compensation. Alun Richards, the playwright, exquisitely summed up the grief – and the relief: 'He was an imp as well as a genius, a scream as well as a sage, a ne'er-do-well as far as possessions were concerned, a charitable soup kitchen all on his own when it came to the persons who sat next to him at functions or dinners – these he fed from his own plate under the tablecloth for he had the appetite of a bored aristocrat, and things he cared for not at all. He once left his car awkwardly parked in my house for a month, returned unexpectedly, gravely opened the boot and presented me with a loaf of home-baked bread and a half a pound of farm butter as a reward. You could have converted neither.

'Those who knew him well know how much he suffered from the incurable and cruel skin disease which meant that he had not had an unbroken night's sleep in years. It was his cross and, I believe, the lack of sleep finally wore him out. He never complained, never referred to it; learned finally to ignore it.'

How I wished I had known the full extent of his suffering. I thought back to our recent meeting. There had been no need for him to come out of his way just to talk to me, to set me on the right lines for this book. In a moving *Guardian* obituary David Frost wrote that 'Carwyn's inability to decline any request to talk to rugby men, to speak at a dinner or to coach at a minor or junior club side contributed to his untimely death.' He had wasted half a day talking to me in a pub near Abergavenny. There was nothing in it for him. Just kindness. And now he was dead. And I, with shaming, criminal selfishness, was annoyed with myself that I had not concentrated more on what he was saying that day, or taken a tape recorder so as to be able to replay Carwyn James's final gems.

He had, I remembered, been reasonably confident that Wales this season might have all the makings, if the selectors were bold enough in a couple of crucial positions. But, oh dear, *what* positions?

I particularly remember his talking of the summer's tour of New Zealand by the British Lions. He had rattled off a few names of those he'd love to do well this season and be picked out of the hat in March by Willie-John. But now I could not recall a single one. And the captain? I wonder who Carwyn would have gone for? Now, two days before 1983's opening international matches I was off to see a front-runner as Lions' leader.

Peter Wheeler was not, of course, captain of England. Yet his highly successful stewardship of the Leicester club and his experience of two Lions' tours already made him the outstanding favourite among the players to lead the British Lions side. Steve Smith himself had told me on Sunday that he reckoned there was no question that Wheeler would be given the job. 'And he's playing better than ever too. Even his throwing into the line-out is near perfect: he's just what the Lions need: as tough as buggery on the field and gentlemanly and beautifully mannered off it.' After watching training at St Mary's teachers' college I went back to the England team's Richmond hotel to have a drink with Peter.

Crucially, he will undoubtedly be worth his place in the Test side. He has been considered by friend and foe as probably the world's best all-round hooker – in the tight, the loose, and as a line-out thrower – for a year or two now; but also as ambassador, after-dinner speaker, respecter of persons, cheerleader, enthusiast and wit, having the character and stamina necessary for probably the most taxing 'official' job in the game. McBride, the tour manager, is well aware of what the job demands, and well aware of Wheeler's qualities. The last stoker-captain to lead the Lions to a series victory while his head was burrowed deep in the boiler-room of the scrum was Willie-John himself, in 1974. In fact, Wheeler was reserve for McBride's team then, even though he had not yet been capped for England. He first pulled on the white jersey a year later, and since 1978 has been a permanent fixture, just as John Pullin had been before him. It's been hard luck for other good hookers for sixteen years.

He is embarrassed at being in the forefront of speculation about the Lions' captaincy. 'Play it down a bit, can't you?' It was very difficult to, I said: he would so obviously make a very good fist of it. Ciaran Fitzgerald,

Ireland's doughty, warrior-like Brian Boru, is also fancied, though relevantly he is not considered anything like as good a hooker as Wheeler. Fitzgerald would win the vote only on his unquestioned powers of leadership: he has done wonders with Ireland. He is a combative, hunky player in the loose, for sure, but many experts would rate him – even while captaining Ireland to their Triple Crown last year – as the worst international hooker in the five nations Championship. For speed about the field, for the instinct of the right place to make for, both in attack and defence, and for the actual technique of low packing, meaty pushing, and fast striking, the Scot, Deans – while in the confessional admitting best to Wheeler – would rightly fancy himself as a better player than Fitzgerald. Not the least skill a hooker must have these days is the accuracy of a cricketer like Underwood at throwing the ball into the line-out. Deans and Wheeler almost pioneered this art.

The England player is now thirty-four, so the end is nigh, and just to go on his third Lions' tour as a player would put a triumphant seal to his career. Wheeler's favourite actress is Glenda Jackson; his favourite actor is Andy Haden, New Zealand's thespian line-out star, who 'fell' out of the line to win the All Blacks their famous last-minute penalty against Wales. His favourite food is bubble and squeak – as you see, he's also a very good interviewee – and his wife is Margaret and they have two baby sons. Sometimes he thinks he would like four more sons, so he could captain a full Wheeler side at the Middlesex Sevens around the year 2,005.

Everyone says he gets better with each big match he plays, and looks even fitter too. In one breath he says that training has become a bit of a drag, but then admits to never skipping a Leicester training evening on Monday night or Thursday – having driven home the twelve miles from the city to Ragdale to help put the boys to bed. And then, if he has a spare lunch hour, you can often catch him whipping round to the Leicester ground in his businessman's suit, changing at speed, and knocking off fifty or sixty sprints up and down the steep terracing bank.

He is an insurance broker with Hogg Robinson. He was born in the south London sprawl, at Norwood. His father was a newsagent and tobacconist at Crofton Park. After the John Ruskin, a soccer school, Peter went to Brockley County. At the very first games lesson he was told to 'go and stand between those two big boys over there'. So he was a hooker from day one. Everything else seems to have been equally cut and dried. He left school at sixteen with five O levels and went straight from the careers master's office to an interview with Lloyds in the City. Start tomorrow, lad! He played three years for the Old Brockleians and was just thinking about having a go with Blackheath when the firm transferred him to Leicester. And that was that.

No one is nearer the heat of the battle than the hooker. 'There's a lot of mystique grown up about what goes on between front rows, and some props like to perpetuate the "secret society" freemasonry of it. Yet the fact remains that it is a very complex area and all to do with weight, balance and leverage. Up and down, round this way and that, forward and back . . .' The hooker has to sustain a tremendous weight on his neck and shoulders. He is, if you like, pinned to a wall by the back of his belt, with his shoulders forward and dropped and his head just a couple of feet from the ground. The signal by the hooker to the scrum-half via a tap on the prop's shoulder is employed by everyone now, which makes heels against the head a rare commodity.

'Striking against the head has become the equivalent of banging your head against a brick wall; now the thing is to help push and make it an eight-man shove or cause disruption by wheeling. Also gone therefore are the "craftsmen" tight heads, the ballplayers with all the tricks and a quick foot like Keith Fairbrother or Micky Burton.' Dirty play has seldom bothered him. What sometimes happens early on when the mighty stags first lock horns is, say, a prop 'coming in' on the hooker. 'We have to show we're not intimidated. We have to establish our ground rules quickly. Referees needn't intervene: we sort it out ourselves pretty sharpish.'

Of the dangers in a scrum collapse, Peter says: 'All you need is a law that the scrummage should be one metre off the ground, or whatever. Every ref in the country could then measure it on his own legs and so stand by each scrum to check its height. It would then make it obvious if someone was pulling the scrum down.'

I recall touring with the Lions for their first month in South Africa in 1980, and was relieved to come home to Britain after the first Test match in Capetown. There is an overlying pall of sadness there: the regime is cruel and undeniably racist. It is definitely not the place for decent, liberal sportsmen to play games in and I felt at the time that Wheeler was of the same mind. He says he still thinks long and hard about South Africa: 'When you're there, you wonder whether you're kidding yourself because it's a lovely place for a white rugby player to go to. For the first half of the 1980 Lions' tour I thought, ugh! what a good window-dressing job they've done just to get us here. But then as the tour went on I became more and more convinced that we were meeting enough average South African whites who were really genuine about seeking change, and were desperate for it to happen before it was too late. Obviously, some Afrikaners weren't, mind you! The government there is a much harder nut to crack, but there is no evidence, is there, that when sports teams from abroad *didn't* go that it had any effect on government? If I was asked to go again, and I said "no", well, they'd take someone else, wouldn't they? Anyway, on balance I think we Brits can now do some good by going.'

Bobby Windsor, hooker supremo of the Viet Gwent, is the best opponent he remembers, and Phil Bennett the very best back he has played with or against. Bennett was Wheeler's first Lions captain. 'Phil was a marvellously nice bloke. In New Zealand he was so homely and homesick that we could all relate to him, work for him, this truly brilliant player who was really just a family man at heart.' I wonder if the same may be said of

A Hotel in Amsterdam

Peter Wheeler come the end of New Zealand's winter.

I would love to have time to research the experts' New Year's day forecasts over the years of the probable Lions' side for the spring – and see how it compared with the actual selection. I bet it would be mighty different. As regards the 1983 captaincy, Wheeler's advantage at this stage over his obvious rival, Fitzgerald, hinged on the Englishman being infinitely better as a hooker. By the same token, nobody was giving Smith an earthly for the post – inspiring tour leader as he might be – because the Welsh scrum-half, Terry Holmes, would surely have Willie-John's team built around him. Holmes himself seemed to have no pretensions to captaincy, nor did the other man almost certainly pencilled into the side, the delicate Irish bootboy, Ollie Campbell. An unknown quantity was the new Welsh captain, Eddie Butler. We would see in the next month or two what he was made of. A stirring season by England's John Scott could push him towards the captaincy. He is most people's certainty to be the Lions' No. 8 – and he has been a rousing leader of Cardiff. In Scotland, Andy Irvine, that electrically charged bright spark at full-back, would have been a likely Lions' captain till he decided earlier in the season not to contemplate even his fourth tour for Britain. Then, only last week, Andy was first deposed as the Scottish leader by Roy Laidlaw, then was forced to cry off from the team itself for the opening match against Ireland. He has a lingering Achilles tendon injury, and with the cultured Rutherford also injured Scotland's high hopes have perforce been lowered some-what. But early days, early days . . .

CHAPTER FIVE

Adventures in the Shin Trade

One of the pities of an international rugby union season these days is that one cannot see every match in person. Two games are played on the same day. Given a choice, one must take pot luck. Having seen the French in Toulouse I thought it made sense to await their arrival at Twickenham – but I knew that this Saturday my mind more than once would drift up to Murrayfield in the gloaming and wonder how their battle was raging. Ireland had retained their grand old guard that won them the Triple Crown last year – the likes of Moss Keane and Willie Duggan and Fergus Slattery. I hoped they would do well enough to retain their places for me to catch up with them during the Championship. Come what may, my pilgrimage was going to take in all those great cathedrals – Lansdowne Road, the Arms Park, Murrayfield and the Parc des Princes. It remained to decide in what order my visits would be.

The French arrived in London two days before the match. Jean Pierre Rives had been picked as captain, of course, although he had played only three first class games since October, including the one in which he had been injured against the Argentinians. They stayed the Thursday night at an airport hotel before moving into central London. Rives had had a haircut, of sorts. Perhaps he had been in mind of the reason some years ago the chairman of the French selectors shruggingly gave for the omission of that joyous, silky centre-threequarter from Perpignan, Jo-Jean Maso: 'Maso has long hair – long hair is for French women, not French rugby players.' If you could get any collective vibes from this newly-arrived side it was one of hushed edginess. Nothing like the cheer of Toulouse. Jean-Pierre intimated that it would be 'very difficult' for me to come and watch them practice. I think the coach, Jacques Fouroux, had suggested to him that I was a spy for the home side.

Instead I went to see the English put a final polish on their preparations at St Mary's College. All remained relaxed and confident. Smith gave a sparkling press conference. 'It's got to happen this year. The time is right now. If we don't click this year we've all missed the boat.' Mike Davis, the coach, said the result of most internationals these days turned on tiny things – minor infringements that gave penalties away and momentary lapses in concentration. 'We have worked very hard at eliminating silly mistakes and errors.' He looked hale and in good heart. The chairman of the selectors, Budge Rogers, kept his own counsel and gave no more away than the usual football managers' clichés at this time – 'the press-ure's on them; we hope just to go out and enjoy ourselves' stuff. More and more, Rogers makes me look up that definition of him by Geoffrey Nicholson in the *Observer* some time ago – 'most people's idea of the clean-cut Englishman: strong vertical features; short, almost school-boyish hairstyle; neck slightly extended for supporting college scarves; a matey open manner, though with certain well-defined no-go areas of conversation.'

Rogers and Davis were stalwarts of the England pack more than a decade ago. Davis won sixteen caps between 1963 and 1970, Rogers over twice as many from 1961. They both knew about over-confidence – and they both knew more about losing than winning. Both of them, however, left the stage just before England embarked on certainly their most dismal decade of the century. The English twentieth-century record goes like this:

	P	W	D	L
1900–09	34	11	2	21
1920–9	40	28	3	9
1930–9	32	16	4	12
1950–9	40	21	6	13
1960–9	40	15	10	15

For the 1970s, the 'League' table reads:

					Points
Wales	39	30	2	7	62
France	40	22	5	13	49
Ireland	38	14	2	22	30
Scotland	39	13	2	24	28
England	40	11	3	26	25

The 1970s try-scoring table underlines how the Lilywhites languished:

	Tries		Penalties	
	F	A	F	A
Wales	93	36	76	68
France	70	45	49	72
Ireland	43	53	62	66
Scotland	51	79	63	62
England	43	89	64	46

They did, at least, give away the fewest scoring penalties.

For the 1980 international season Rogers took over as chairman of the selectors and Davis, who had been a successful eminence with the England Schools XV, became coach. Bill Beaumont's side promptly won the Grand Slam – beating, literally, all comers. Since when the English have had an allowable presumption of victory – and rheumy-eyed old codgers in army greatcoats up in the stand have, with one hand, taken swigs from their hip flasks in celebration while, with the other, sought out under the tartan travelling rug the knee or even withered thigh of their white-faced spouse and brought with a loving squeeze the rouge rushing to the lady's haughty cheeks for probably the first time since VE night. Or at least since Macmillan's 1959 election victory.

Ah, Twickenham. It would be nice to say the old place has not changed, but the romantic's open South Bank has been replaced by a snazzy, two-tiered stand in the modern wavy-concrete idiom; it tones in with the rest of the famous stadium as would a Post Office Tower plonked alongside Salisbury's serene and lovely spire. For the rest, it remains Twickenham; lush green grass and faded green woodwork; officers' Mess for the middle classes. Half a century ago Alec Waugh wrote: 'An international at Twickenham is more than a mere spectacle. It is the gathering of the clan.' John Morgan has described, 'at Waterloo Station the flat caps, the duffle coats, the accents that mark a man from Kuala Lumpur to Salisbury, all moving, the middle-class masses, towards Platform 19; in the car park the Bentleys and the TR3s; and along the touchline the screaming boys in blazers and in the stands the men with unmistakeable faces and the pretty women in camelhair coats; how did the middle classes manage before Twickenham was built?'

'Twickers', a sporting arena in a Surrey suburb that gave its name to a type of chap, was the brainchild of Billy Williams, a carefree batchelor, who lived down the road at Walpole House at the turn of the century. England were then playing their rugby matches in Bristol or the north, or at Crystal Palace or Richmond. Williams heard the Mann family of market gardeners wanted to sell their orchards alongside the Crane River at Twickenham. He persuaded the autocratic old treasurer of the Rugby Union, William Cail, to cough up £5,572.12.6d for the ten-acre site. The ground is still known affectionately as 'Billy Williams' cabbage patch'. A better name might have been 'Fields of Cail', for it was Cail who raised the loot – and the quality of the bargain he had struck was seen when in 1924, the last year of his RFU office, he had to pay five times as much, £25,000, for an extra seven acres for, as he minuted, 'parking grounds for motors'.

If Williams and Cail built Twickenham as a temple to the gentlemanly, amateur, leisurely-but-Spartan spirit of Edwardian sport then nowhere is such a caste and cast-list more evoked than in its car parks before an international match. Snifters are sizeable, and start at eleven. By noon, from the boots of those Bentleys and TR3s, are brought hot soups and cold chickens, piping pigeon pie and chilli con carne and I say, botheration, I've forgotten the corkscrew.

I mooched around, catching the odd eye and acquiring the odd drink. It was biting cold and the wind was blustery, but it was good to be back. Now, where was I this time last year? Madras, where Vishy got his 222 and Botham went bananas? . . . No, we'd left Madras by now . . . it must have been Calcutta, where Boycott played his last Test in front of 85,000 and Botham again went bananas, but this time with the bat. It was as good to have been there as to be at Twickenham now. Twickenham and international rugby union first wheedled its way into my consciousness, courtesy of the old *Daily Graphic*, in a freezing prep school common room. Photographers in those days obviously sat in the stand, for every Monday morning we had wide-angled pictures of half the pitch with arrows and dotted lines to explain the fuzzy action of man and ball. The *Graphic* was especially graphic (why, for heavens sake, can't the sporty Snowdons do a bit of that now? A close-up zoom lens picture of a few straining thighs in a ruck or line-out may be art but it does not tell the story: if Obolensky scored his try now it would probably be captured for immortality by a close-up of an out-of-focus Russian earhole to denote a Tartar's speed).

As a boy, I remember, I had been thrilled with the bullocking runs of Woodward, the Wycome butcher against Bob Scott's All Blacks. It was from a scrum on the same touchline whence Clarke fed Richard Sharp for his classical fly-half's try against Scotland in 1965. Both Mike Davis and Budge Rogers were playing that day. I wasn't there, but I remember it well for I was doing a Saturday afternoon shift on the Gloucester *Citizen* 'Pink' Un' and the teatime tapes from Twickenham were chattering away like piano chopsticks at the very excitement of it. Brace and Smith I recalled, as ever, with affection too: it would have been even more perfect if one or other of the duo had set a seal to that day with a riveting try. I suppose the best two tries of my lifetime on this ground – Obolensky's in 1936 was eighteen months before I was born – were wingers' last-minute jobs: Peter Jackson's dragonfly dash, going south down the west touch-line, against the Aussies in 1958; and, in the opposite direction, Andy Hancock's madcap, marathon eighty-yarder to beat Scotland in 1965. I seem to remember hearing both of those scores described – hoarsely – on the wireless.

The best try I ever saw here was in 1969 by a superb young runner in the centre, one David Duckham. I remember his first try at Twickenham, a daring pass and loop with his winger in his first Calcutta Cup game. In the next season came his, mine and everyone's favourite – that coruscating sprint against the dreaded Springboks, fair hair streaming like a pre-Raphaelite angel, winged boots always no more than an inch from the left touchline till he ducked inside the murderous cover of De Villiers with no more than a shrug of a hip.

'From ten yards away,' said Mervyn Davies once, 'David's sidestep looked obvious and predictable, but when you were there in close up it had you stranded and leaden-footed.' Mervyn complimented few Englishmen.

Duckham, alas, and through no fault of his own – unless being too gentlemanly, meek and patient was a fault of Englishmen on the rugby field – then had his mettle and his talent corroded by England's long years in the wilderness through the 1970s. When David retired, exactly ten years after those first languid, lyrical Corinthian's tries, he told me with a sigh: 'In those early days with England there was a totally different attitude. We took far more risks. It was fun. We were allowed scope to dare and scope to enjoy ourselves, try things. Then attitudes changed. International rugby seemed to become too intense; you had to win. Everything was stamped with a no-risk policy.'

Had the weakened squad coaching, the blackboard jumble of attacking arrows and defensive dots, the nine-man rugby, the ten-man rugby, the No. 8-man rugby, the crash ball, the ruck ball, the tight ball, the fight maul . . . had it all, in Duckham's dozen years, ruined a beautiful game? No, I don't think so. It had just made it different, made it if anything more of a team but less of an individual's sport. These thirty young men from France and England, clad in their snazzy, officially sponsored, badged and tailored tracksuits (shades of Stack Stevens's jeans!) were going through there 'learning' routines one last time as they laced their boots over their under the Royal Box – down in the Twickenham dungeons. Keep it tight, lads, keep it tight! No mistakes, lads, no mistakes! No wonder no one was going to dare – though 70,000 were here just in case they did.

Both these sides have spent five days together out of the last eight. When Richard Sharp first played at fly-half for England he had never met his scrum-half, Dick Jeeps, let alone received a pass from him. I remember Dr Tommy Kemp, England's fine fly-half a dozen years before Sharp, telling me once of *his* match day preparation: 'I would get up early on the big day, go for a run, put in a hard morning's work at St Mary's, then rush to Waterloo and travel down on the crowded train to Twickenham carrying my boots.'

Only twenty years ago just before the kick-off an Irish forward knocked on the door of the England dressing-room holding one boot and, after asking his rivals if any of them had 'so much as a length of hairy twine to serve as a lace', went out wishing the opposition 'all the very best of luck to you, lads'. Now these two 1983 teams were waiting for the call from the dressing-room as tense as boxers might be before a million-dollar prize fight.

One last cadge in the car park. The *Daily Mail* always bag the corner nearest the turnstile and O'Connor and Wooldridge are generous hosts. The toasts were sad and for Carwyn. Also there was another friend, the American in Paris, Bob Donahue, a rugby buff in Twickenham's statutory Dorking duffle; his beat is the boulevards, for he works for the *International Herald Tribune*. He already knew the match result. 'Being on speaking terms, more or less, with my newspaper's computer, I asked it who would win. FRANCE BY FIVE POINTS came the startling reply. This seemed too good to be true, so I poked about in the surly machine's tapes until I finally pieced together the simple equation. You may recall that poor Canada lost by thirty-five points (35–0) to Argentina not long ago, and then by thirty-seven points (43–6) to England. These numbers fancy England by two points over Argentina, whom France recently beat (13–6) by seven points. Now you know.'

What about the Championship? 'It says France will finish on top with seven championship points, ahead of Scotland and Wales with four, Ireland with three and England with only two. Of course, it's an American computer, resident in Paris. As such, it may be slightly prejudiced!' We shall see.

The roar at Twickenham is substantial enough: it sails up to rattle the rafters and then away with the swirling winds: it is perhaps not so much a roar as a beery or brandified bray that urges the flower of England not to wilt, to keep upper lips stiff and chins up. Sometimes, like today, there's a confident tinge of presumption and arrogance about it; oftentimes in the recent past its crescendoes have faded away to sighs in desperation.

In the absence of Phil Blakeway, the first battalion of the Gloucestershire Regimental Band – a good omen? – played 'The British Grenadiers' and 'Land of Hope and Glory' immediately before the national anthems. Rives ran out first, then waited just inside the touchline to give each of his men a word and a slap on the rump. Smith won the toss and played with the boisterous wind – a sensible ploy at Twickenham, where the weather-vanes have been known to Strauss-waltz all afternoon. The first crucial three scrums were France's, and within five minutes the blue juggernaut looked, ominously for England, to have settled into a relentless rhythm. Davies made a crucial, lassooing tackle on Esteve, and Blanco had his first excursion into the line as the vast throng held its breath. Camberabero dropped a penalty goal, Hare at once retaliated, then put England ahead with a prodigious job from the halfway line. Both kickers also made regular hashes of better chances. The French front five were formidable, puncturing every likelihood of the English getting up a head of steam: the last leading England quintet I had seen was Blakeway, Wheeler, Cotton, Beaumont, Colclough. Only Peter and big Maurice remained now, and it looked a different game. Just on half-time Hare had another potshot; it might have hit the bar; it wouldn't have cleared it. Blanco, the delightful, zany nut, quite unnecessarily leaped high like a Peter Shilton to 'save' one-handed. It was marvellous. But it was also a knock-on. From the scrum a yard out England held, then heeled – and Cusworth plopped the ball over to give England a 9–3 lead which fooled no one.

There had been nothing to make anyone miss a heartbeat. Now, even more ominously, Colclough was last to the rucks and obviously in pain. Just before half-time one of his own forwards had fallen on his left knee: it was already swathed in elastic bandages. He ambled away sadly and Hesford, of Bristol, came on, to play out of position at lock. He must have wondered what hit him: suddenly the French were dancing, a-buzz in a swarm: within quarter of an hour 9–3 to England had become 19–9 to France.

Thirty yards out, in front of the posts, Rodriguez broke left from a set scrum. Winterbottom was late to spot him: the Frenchman brushed little Cusworth aside and fed Martinez. Camberabero was half-through, half-tackled, but squirted the ball out to the enthusiastically looping Martinez, and two fingertip transfers gave the sprinter Esteve a clear run. Blanco converted. Nine-all. Now the Whites were grey and the Blues winking-bright neon. A long throw on England's line. Joinel palms, Paparemborde peels from the front, and the bullet-headed battering ram hits poor brave Cusworth amidships as Rives and the rest of the French pack joyously but needlessly help Papa over. Blanco converts again: 9–15. The light kept winking: an orthodox move from a line-out, Blanco in the line, Dodge just gets his ankles as he ghosts by, Davies overshoots, and Sella picks up the ball round his bootlaces but still has time to run at Swift – zig in, zag out, and over by inches in the corner. 9–19. That's that. The French drop back into second gear, England try and run everything, but in truth they are frayed at the edges and Hare's two late penalty kicks will only make the thing seem close when grandchildren come across it in *Rothmans Rugby Yearbook*.

The first man I saw in the Committee Room corridor was Willie-John McBride. 'Sure it was very disappointing for England; it was also very disappointing for me.' Before the match he might have pencilled in perhaps a dozen Englishmen for his Lions. After this his Christmas list would be looking pretty limp. McBride's biggest blow must have been the news of Colclough. The eighteen-stoner was already 'on the table' at the West Middlesex Hospital, having a ruptured medial ligament sewn together by Iain Duff, the Rugby Union's doctor. It was serious; he was out for the season and probably for the summer as well.

Steve Smith showered at speed. He, too, was distressed about Colclough. 'Inside a year we've lost the two best locks in the world in Billy and Maurice.' He admitted England had been 'reasonably stuffed on the day – we never settled, they never let us settle.' Still, he said, that's France out of the way. 'We can still win the Triple Crown, don't forget.' The smile was back in place. After all, it was only a game, wasn't it? Davis, the tracksuited coach, looked sad. 'There were enough good things we did to build on for our remaining games, but we snatched at too much and simply hoped that bobbing balls might bounce our way.' Rogers, the selector, looked stern in his club tie and his cav. twills – 'you say nobody actually played very badly, but I'll tell you, nobody actually played very well.' He was gracious to the French – just as the French leader was soon to be gracious to the vanquished.

Outside Wales Jean-Pierre Rives must surely be rugby's most famous J.P.R. of all. He is leader both temporal and spiritual; emperor as well as gladiator; both combatant and philosopher. His whole team had run to embrace him at the end. He had a quick shower, after which the water

Swift has Sella in his sights. The darting French sprinter has zigged inwards, now zags out, and Swift, out of position on the left-wing, cannot quite pinion him at the corner flag. England's discarded left-winger, Slemen, was to say later: 'If I'd been playing, I'd have got him.' And most people at Twickenham would have agreed with him.

was still dripping off his flaxen hair. It dampened the shoulders of his black blazer, but the yellow cockerel on the breast-badge still chortled. J.P.R. fingered the egg-size lump between his eyebrows and mused on the age-old sporting conundrum. Why, for no apparent reason, can it sometimes go right just as easily as it can go wrong? The mood is all.

Once the French could never express themselves on London's rugby field. Rives has changed all that. Before the game he said in his most glorious pidgin English: 'I larve to be in your Twicken-Ham, I do know why, so well.' He nursed the egg at the top of his patrician's nose – fingertipping it like a housewife in the market place determining if an avocado was 'just so' – and settled into his parley: 'Ah, *oui*, I larve Twicken-Ham. Perhaps for me it is just the greenness of it. Everything is green. I like it. I like it as well when opponent never know 'ow we will play. I like when *we* never know 'ow we will play. I like when *all* the French people never know 'ow we will play.'

What's French for 'Getting out of bed on the right side'? His eyes dart, and he smiles as he searches for reasons: 'This morning I just have the feeling, the same I have here at London some year ago: "We have an 'atmosphere', an atmosphere 'sensitif'." We 'ope *naturellement* to find the same atmosphere like today for the next three games; but 'oo can tell? Sometimes you discover it, sometime you do not. It is not our decision – atmosphere is made by someone else.'

He points expressively to heaven, smiles and shrugs . . . and remembers how France last beat England at Twickenham, in 1981. His philosopher's tale went something like this: 'The morning of the match we have breakfast in the hotel in Mayfair. After, we go for a run in the park nearby. Under a tree there is an empty old sardine tin. We start to kick it around as football, I remember, and then to pass it about in our 'ands. Now this morning in 1983, do you know, the very same thing 'appens. After breakfast we jog . . . and there is a sardine tin under the very same tree. And we kick it around and throw it together – and then I realise the atmosphere is "*très, très sensitif*".' And when the game starts, 'I know it is still "*sensitif*".

' 'ow,' asked Jean-Pierre, 'the result in Edinbeurre?' Ireland won, we told him, by 15–13. 'They both,' said Jean-Pierre, fingering his egg, 'will be vaire, vaire difficult.' Ireland, in fact, did extremely well to hang on to their narrow lead. Next afternoon I watched the video recording on BBC-2's *Rugby Special*. The wind was cruel and, if anything, the line-out play of the Irish jumper, Lenihan, might have swung the thing – plus, of course, Fitzgerald's wayward throwing in. Ollie Campbell, it goes without saying, kicked Ireland into a 15–4 half-time lead with the zephyrs zapping like crazy behind him – also converting a lovely sprinter's try by

---

The Welsh dragonfly decides his course. The very moment Clive Rees comes off his left foot at Murrayfield after his thrilling touchline dash. It ended in one of the tries of the year – in the opposite corner.

Kiernan who followed up to skid on to Finn's gorgeously-timed kick ahead. Scotland's four points in the first half came when Laidlaw, that impressive bundle of sinew at scrum-half, broke obliquely from a scrum to leave the Irish pack looking as old as they are. Thereafter, however, the old men marshalled their forces and their nerves to fight a magnificently controlled rearguard action in the closing stages.

Dods, deputising for Irvine, started nervously, but improved by the minute. He kicked two penalty goals in the second half and Renwick dropped a goal to put just two points in it. Twenty minutes remained: Scotland pressed in a frenzy, Ireland defended their line with heroic resolution. Hugo MacNeill at full-back stood firmest of all, though in the dying minutes the winning strike was manufactured, on instinct, by the old warhorse, Fergus Slattery, when instead of tackling he charged down Renwick's drop kick under the posts that would have won the game for Scotland by a single point. Hooray, I thought selfishly; the Irish selectors would be happy and I would be able to see 'Dad's Army' in action yet.

Ireland had five weeks to rest and recuperate before their next match – France at Lansdowne Road. In three weekends, Scotland would travel to Paris and England to Wales. In between was England's County Championship final: Gloucestershire at home to Yorkshire. In the past thirteen seasons Gloucestershire had contested an astonishing ten finals. In the eight successive years from 1970 they won four, lost four. No county this century has bettered Gloucester's thirteen outright titles. Yorkshire were last in the final twenty years ago; they last won all of thirty years before.

From the *Stroud News* and *Hereford Times*, both weeklies, I had graduated, briefly, to the bigtime – an evening paper. Though I was then a sub-editor on general news – Women's Institute expert, flower shows a speciality – we were expected to help put the Saturday sports 'Pink 'Un' to bed. County rugger Saturdays were very special editions. On those afternoons the *Gloucester Citizen* employed extra boys to race the 'running' paragraphs from the Kingsholm press box; a dash down Dean's Walk, a hare up Hare Lane with a breathless skid into the sports editor's tray in St John's Lane. The world was waiting. And 'the world' then meant the *Citizen*'s sister 'Pinks', at Cheltenham and Bristol. Is the *Citizen* still the only Pink in Britain invariably to lead its front page with rugby? 'Where do you want Cinderford v Coney Hill to go?' I would ask the sports editor, furiously attacking a scrap of ill-typed paper with my biro. '*Front!*' he would scream. And later, 'What page Manchester United v Spurs, sir?' 'Page six,' he would mumble dismissively.

By the tag-end of the fifties I was working on that same southerly sister, the *Bristol Evening World*. It was like yesterday that I was sweating on the runner of the 1959 final as the paragraph came into the office from the Memorial Ground. We were leading the match until near the end and I had even written the headline, 'GLOSHIRE DO IT!' – then the last flash came through telling of Warwickshire's final try and the nail being hammered in by George Cole of the boot. That was the start of Warwickshire's seven titles in eight years. Nobody has bettered that mighty spasm. But 'Glorse' have come close.

Oddly enough, Gloucestershire won their first final against Yorkshire – in 1910. In my day, you could still meet old men in pubs who would reverently place their pint pot on a table, lower their eyes, and recite the team that day: 'Johnson, Hudson, Spoors, Neale, Eberle' (pause for a sip, then even more reverence), 'Dai Gent and Jimmy Stephens'. (Another swig before the pack would come out in an eightsome rush): 'Johns, Berry, Uzzell, 'Olford and 'Ollands, Gardner, Wright 'n Bowkett.' Gloucester won that game 23–0 and contemporary reports began, 'It was a beautiful spring day and the ground was in tip-top condition . . .'

Gloucestershire's tradition – in which they exult, sometimes boringly – has been of rough, tough forwards, fist-happy thickoes from the Forest of Dean or from the bleak midwinter villages on the hills above the Severn plain. Yet I was privileged to be in on John Blake's running team at Bristol in the fifties and sixties. What a man! He revolutionised the game long before new rules could. As a fly-half he had to run – because he could not kick. Week after week he inspired his mates to run with him through every tackler as though all fifteen of them were demented electronic pinballs. Blake's Bristol XV scored try upon glorious try. An England selector once came down to pick him for Twickenham but sadly pronounced – 'Brilliant he is, but how can a man play for England if he cannot kick?'

Gloucestershire rugby more than most owes its strength and historical eminence to the small clubs from which it feeds so voraciously. Time without number have I scanned the names of the latest county selection and despairingly read the parenthesis 'Gloucester' or 'Bristol'. We exiles want to know where a new lad learned his game – in Longlevens, Lydney or Cheltenham, in Stroud or Clifton or Cirencester, or Cainscross or the Gordon League, or Painswick, or Pates or St Pauls . . . But, simply, if you want to play for the county you have got to join Bristol or Gloucester.

In their centenary brochure a few years back the Stroud club reflected: 'If there is a weakness in Gloucestershire rugby it lies in the fact that in the last two or three seasons Bristol and Gloucester, because of their successes on the field of play, have attracted to their ranks more good players than they need. A place on the touchline as a travelling reserve or a run around in the "United" is no training ground for the modern game. This is not knocking at our old friends, Bristol and Gloucester. It is vital to the game in the county that they should be strong. It is equally vital that Stroud, Lydney, Cheltenham and Clifton should be strong.'

I was once 'attracted' to Gloucester. Having brought me up midway between the shrine at Kingsholm and one of its attendant altars, at Fromehall in Stroud, my father went and did a daft thing: he sent me away to school – and not only that, but a school in the dreaded Home

Counties. A rugger establishment, sure. But not at all the same thing as a Gloucestershire rugger school.

So a fancypants scrum-half came back to Gloucester in the middling 1950s. My first-hand experience – or rather *second*, for I was surely concussed most of the time – did not last very long. I probably had the shortest 'career' in big-time sport since another local lad, Sam Cook, the Tetbury plumber and left-handed bowler, played his one single Test match for England – nought for plenty against South Africa in 1947.

Anyway, armed with a letter and encouragement from our rugby master at school to continue my rugby career, I turned up for late-summer training trials at Kingsholm. Yes, I thought, aim for the top, bypass Stroud and Cainscross. I turned up in Persilled shorts and gleaming new Cotton-Oxfords. That was my first mistake. I saw a diabolic gleam in the eye of Peter Ford as I was introduced in the locker room – he was a destroyer of half-backs for England as well as for Gloucestershire. My second mistake was to allow myself to be picked on the opposite side to Peter in the muck-around touch rugby game that followed the training session. *Touch* rugby! The first time I touched the ball Mr Ford, my marker, compressed me to the earth like a flea under a copper's foot. I was scraped up, rolled to the touchline and left for dead.

Years later, browsingly reviewing the rugby autobiography of one of Ford's apprentices around that time, that amiable hard nut with the soft centre, Mike Burton, I found myself breaking into a shiver. This is what Burton wrote about a typical Gloucester pre-match team talk: 'Mickey

'Andy Morris, Rumney seconds, blindside trampling. What are you in for?'

No more hassles, either mental or physical. Both Gloucester and England's first setback came when their doughty fruit n' veg merchant, Colin Blakeway, called it a day. 'I'm just fed up with the bump and grind of it all,' said the man from the county that, some said, invented bump and grind in the first place!

Booth, who was captain, would pass among us uttering gruff, mumbling noises. When we were ready, Booth would address the assembly. "Just give me the ball," he would say. "I want you donkeys to give me the ball and I'll do the rest. Anything to say, Peter?" He always called on the experienced Ford. The man himself stood up, glistening and toothless. "Just good old-fashioned stuff. Get in and 'it 'em hard" – one of the precepts of the Gloucester legend. Ford was ruthless, and under the old rules which allowed flankers to creep round scrums he made the lives of many scrum-halves a misery.'

Anyway, that touch rugby night at Kingsholm saw me helped home by Russell Hillier, a Stroudite who *could* stand the heat and, indeed, went on to play for the county. Next morning I had to be driven to Dr Kinsella's surgery in Stonehouse. He laughed, too, and said I had all the symptoms of shellshock. Gloucester never sent me another postcard – and when I telephoned them to ask when I could come and collect my boots a man suggested that if I was still keen on having an occasional game 'then I should give Stroud Nomads a ring'. So I never did get to hear Peter Ford's longest speech – before a county semi-final: 'If it's dark and moves kick it; it might be the ball. If it's dark and still just stand on it. If it squeals, say "Sorry" in earshot of the ref.'

What a player Ford was! Coincidentally, his one international season for England was in 1964 in an untechnical era of fast and loose, destructive flankers – and he packed down alongside Mike Davis and Budge Rogers, now respectively England's coach and chairman of selectors. Blimey, what sort of England coach would Peter Ford have made! His combative philosophies would have made establishments quake.

Higgledy-piggledy, Gloucester names trip off the tongue as I write . . . Hook and Hall and Hudson and Hastings and Hopson and Haines; Terrington and Ibbotson, Jones and Nicholls; Watkins and Smith and Fowke; Booth and Blakeway and Boughton and Burton and Bayliss and Brinn and Boyle and Butler . . . but I suppose the most shining light in the legend, top of the roll of honour, remains Tom Voyce, who played for England through the 1920s. The All Blacks came over in 1925, bone-hard, closed-knuckles, mean-eyed and nasty. Certainly they looked to get their retaliation in first – and certainly the opening quarter-hour of the Twickenham international was mind-boggling in its explosive dirtiness. Then Voyce – already with a cut eye and lip – turned to Wavell Wakefield, his battered captain, and said with a grin through the gore, 'Up with your sleeves, my old skip. By golly, it's real good fun, isn't it? I didn't know these buggers went in as hard as this.' I met Tom Voyce once, at a 'do' in a hotel near Amberley. He was an old man, but spry. I asked him if that story was true. He said nothing. But he twinkled and looked pleased.

By then my own 'career' in one of the finest rugby-playing provinces of them all had long been terminated. I did play a couple of games for Stroud Nomads. Then again no more postcards came. When I joined the *Stroud News* as a cub reporter the chief printer was Norman Hall, who was captain of Cainscross. They were looking for a scrum-half like me. So were opposing wing-forwards! One game – and I was then in the Cainscross seconds – against Painswick, trampling, hairy, hillside oiks. The referee that day was Bomber Wells, much-respected Gloucestershire cricketer, who loved his rugger in the winters. After half an hour the Bomber blew shrill his whistle and brought the game to a stop. He ordered my battered body to the wing – or else, he said, when I got my breath back, he would send me off. 'Hey, you can't do that!' said my captain. 'I can,' said Bomber. 'It's to save him from further punishment!' I staggered to the touchline as if it were heaven. For the rest of my life I stuck to cricket.

Yorkshire's vibrant threequarter play all season was far more tidy, trim, and fashionable than their supporters' puddeny headwear. No one could remember if such millinery was worn when last Yorkshire made a final.

Meanwhile, here in 1983, was it me getting old, or had Gloucestershire's self-fostered tradition of amiable toughness on the rugby field gone too far? Were they now not victims of their own publicity? Had rousing forward strength turned into nothing less than sly thuggery? The Gloucester club itself was having a wretched season in every way – not least because, before Christmas, they'd had *three* men already sent off. The last to go, at Bath on 12 December, was Mike Teague, a No. 8 who was in the England squad. No more, for England's strict rule is that any man sent off will not be considered for the rest of the season. An irony is that it looks as though a Gloucester man, Steve Boyle, may well replace the injured Colclough in the second row for England's match against Wales, when it should surely have been given to Jim Syddal, the Waterloo lock; except that Syddal had been sent off against Leicester on 4 December!

So I was going to give a miss to Gloucestershire's county final with

Old enjoys his final fling in his 69th match for Yorkshire – closely watched by Gloucestershire's captain, Mike Rafter.

Yorkshire – of necessity, anyway, for it clashed with the memorial service for Carwyn James at his village Tabernacle up in his beloved hills at Cefn-Eithin. Nevertheless had the dates not been the same I fear I would have discovered in my heart and spirit a sacrilegious taint, for a Glouces-ter man, of harbouring the hope that Yorkshire might win, and win handsomely. And I suspected – indeed, knew – that one or two lifelong 'Glorse-ites' felt the same. Grinding, relentless forward play with a touch of maliciousness is one thing, but Yorkshire had won through to the final as definite underdogs by dint of some tearaway, much yearned-for, three-quarter sparkle. Most of all, any romantic would want to see the veteran, Alan Old, cap his career by leading Yorkshire to their first Championship since 1953. His side was young and fresh and fair – and Old would be making his sixty-ninth appearance for his county. How could anyone not want Yorkshire to win well? At thirty-seven, it would be, said Old, 'the most important game of his life'.

I recalled, too, listening to the crackly transistor static coming across the ocean as Alan's brother Chris and I attempted to hear the World Service rugby commentaries when we were touring with MCC cricket teams. Alan was in and out of England's rugby XV as much as Chris the XI, even though he was acknowledged by most of the game's players to be the best fly-half in the country between, say, 1972 and 1979. But he only played sixteen matches for England, by whom he was dropped and recalled four times. He was given six half-back partners and played alongside eleven different centres.

In an interview just before the final with the *Guardian*'s northern correspondent, David Irvine, Alan put it down in part to bad selection. 'Until the last two seasons the selectors never gave the pack a chance to establish themselves. It's the same with Yorkshire cricket; there's no tolerance or patience with not being the best. Now we're realising that we must find the best player in each position and make an effective unit out of them. You can't build up a representative side by picking a team one week and making four changes the next, particularly when you have not even watched the four players you bring in. That's just hoping – selection by sticking in a pin.'

When he was dropped by England for the third time one of his supporters wrote a long letter to *The Times*, sneering at his successor and arguing the relative strengths and subtleties of Old. The irate correspon-dent then added a PS to the effect that he was sending to each selector 'a copy of this same letter – in Braille'.

Old reminded Irvine how, over the years, he had become something of a favourite with the *Guardian*'s famous gremlins. Once, when he part-nered Roger Pickering, there was a reference to 'Yorkshire's half-backs, old and bickering'. Another time, in a preview to a Roses match which stressed his prowess as a goal-kicker, the headline read: 'Lancs fear old boot.'

I left the West and went deeper westwards, to Wales. We heard the result of the English county final at Llanelli. Gloucester had out-shoved and out-manoeuvred Yorkshire to win by 19–7; but the underdogs had acquitted themselves extremely well in what, by all accounts, was a vibrantly inventive game. It was 7–7 at the interval and only towards the end had Gloucester's relentless power allowed them to pull away on a quagmire of a pitch. Old had played beautifully, but had place-kicked badly.

We witnessed a fine match, too, in which Llanelli deservedly and most appropriately beat Cardiff 16–15 at Stradey. Somewhere up there Carwyn James would doubtless have chuckled, hummed a snatch of Dafydd Iwan and drawn satisfyingly deep on one of his now unlimited supply of free cigarettes at the exuberant performance of possibly his favourite scarlet-vested old boy, Ray Gravell, the bearded warrior who refused to play for Wales any more because of the pain he suffered when they dropped him.

Other former pupils were in the stand. Barry and Gareth and Gerald and Delme, Phil Bennett and Terry Davies and Derek Quinnell . . . An hour or two before they had been up in the hills to genuflect a formal farewell to Carwyn at the service in the Tabernacle at Cefn-Eithin. Police unravelled the traffic. An hour before the service the tiny building was crammed. Many more hundreds filled the neighbouring vestry.

John Reason had written in the *Telegraph*: 'No cathedral in the land would be big enough to hold all those who wanted either to weep for him or to salute him or to nod in respect to a man they may not have known but whom they knew to be something very, very special.'

I was early. Already the central building was full. 'Please,' I said to the man at the door, 'can't you squeeze me in? I'm from the *Guardian*.' Kindly, he said he would try and I was to follow him. No chance, surely. Both aisles were thick with folk. Yet the doorman led me on through the throng – to an inch of space next to a television lamp standard and under the very pulpit itself. 'Make room for this man, please,' he said. 'You see, he's from the *Ammanford Guardian*.'

The white-washed chapel gleamed. Sunday suits were of charcoal grey. All was monochrome, the only two slashes of colour – apart from the oratory to come – a spray of early daffodils and, appropriately again, a big scarlet fire extinguisher near the door. Everyone was there. I recognised Gerald Davies and Barry John, and recalled a snatch of Carwyn's philosophy. He had said once – 'I love an inner calm, a coolness, a detachment; a brilliance and insouciance which is devastating. Like Barry or Gerald. Some sniff the wind – they created it.'

The jostling, whispering scrum grew outside the main door. Over their heads I could see the car park that had been made exactly opposite the Tabernacle on the scanty patch of overgrown ground. The children's swings were rusty now. On one side of the bleak field was Carwyn's little home. On the other side, third council house from the right, was Barry's. Carwyn was the village hero before Barry: 'Whenever he used to trot out on to the park to do some training he was soon surrounded by boys. I was nearly always the first there. We used to run with him, pass to him and kick to him. At times we must have been a nuisance, but he never asked us to go away. Carwyn was a patient man, and no doubt he recalled his own boyhood when he watched Cefn-Eithin as often as he could and earned threepence a game by retrieving the ball from back gardens on the east touchline. After a while he used to take us to one side and squat down and talk to us about rugby. He showed me how to dummy, to side-step, the art he had learned through watching the heroes of *his* youth, like Haydn Jones and Bleddyn Williams.'

And now, a quarter of a century later, in this whitewashed chapel next to that nondescript – but oh, so famous – recreation field, the very heart and whole of the spirit of a grand and worldwide confraternity had gathered. No, even more than that. Television News was there – but for general network consumption, not just for sporting bulletins. Has modern, organised sport thrown up such a man as Carwyn? At one and the same time poet and pragmatist and preacher, practiser and philosopher, wise innocent and melancholic optimist.

Not a word of English was spoken at the service. From the pulpit, in richly melodic Welsh, came wave after wave of lilting tribute and fire-and-brimstone grief. The singing was so sensational that even up in Heaven residents would have had to have turned the sound down.

It was not only sport that grieved and gave thanks. Not by any means. Spellbinding oratory from the Arch Druid offered gratitude from the ancient Celts, and Gwynfor Evans from the dead man's passion, Plaid Cymru. Carwyn's own Mynydd Mawr male voice choir thundered out the responses. The world may have been watching, but this was a private ceremony – the enclosed, exclusive Celtic village paying homage to a favourite villager. I was the interloper, for while the soul was moved I did not understand one word. I would whisper to my neighbour for an English equivalent. They would crease their brow to help, before apologising, 'all lost in the translation, boy.'

Gerald Davies tried, after the stirring magnificence of the hymn 'Calon Lan' had stereoed the senses. *'I do not ask for comforts and riches/Nor earthly treasures of gold or gems/All I need and ask for is a happy heart/A true heart, an honest heart and a pure heart.'* And Ian Edwards, of ITN, helped with the sombre *'Yn ei oes, croes. Yn ei arch, parch'* – *'In his lifetime he bore a cross. In his coffin he won our respect.'*

CHAPTER SIX

Inside the Principality

Though it is only sixty-odd miles from Wales, the honeyed, warm Cotswold stone of the Cheltenham College cloisters is spiritually a million miles away from the slag-black workaday wastes of Pontypool. It is a culture shock to jump in just over an hour from an awfully-awfully English public school in the shires to an industrial 'village' rugby club in the grey and sooty hills of South Wales. Eddie Butler, the new young captain of Wales, bridges that gap at least four times a week.

By day, around the stately halls of Cheltenham, Butler teaches modern languages, general studies and rugby union. In the evenings he is either leading the famed Pontypool pack in a gruelling match – by definition in Wales most fixtures are local derbies – or enduring a draining training session under the command of the club's original and rightly revered coach, Ray Prosser.

The legendary 'Pross' is still bellowing away fifteen to the dozen, still investing the most familiar of four-letter words with a unique and savagely lyrical venom. Eff is the colour. 'No, boy, I still don't believe in using your effing long words like effing "corrugated" or effing "marmalade".' If the headmaster of Cheltenham College knew what sort of company his fresh-faced young language master was keeping he'd have had him up in his study after prep, pronto.

Butler finished his class at about the time the early evening television news was coming on, hurried to his car without pause even to wipe the blackboard chalk from his fingers, bunged his bag in the boot and drove me to his other country, his other culture. Pross greets his protégé with an approving beam. Pontypool's ground, ringed by gloomy hills and phosphorus lights, is a public park. Thus ratepayers can barge through the turnstiles for free if they say they're taking their dog for a walk. Pontypool is the most strongly supported club in the canine world. Now the dogs smell each other or sit patiently by their masters' boots as they watch Pross go through his bullying, belly-aching routines. Within minutes the platoon to a man is rummaging ever more deeply for breath. Their sweat shirts have noticeably darkened. Always Butler is in the frame.

Pontypool is the home and haven and heart of Welsh forward play. They keep it tight there. There was once a joke which went thus:

'They've found Lord Lucan.'

'Where?'

'A very good hiding place – all these years he's been playing on the wing at Pontypool.'

Pross's views are, as ever, emphatic: 'This game's all about effing physical fitness and I'm 'ere to make sure you can't get enough of it.' Ruck and run, ruck and run . . . Agonising, full-pelt circuits . . . ruck and run, ruck and run . . . short sprints and long sprints and murderous, unending press-ups – 'Effin' c'mon, really shake those bollocks up.' Then scrum, scrum and scrum again – 'Hey, boy, if you don't get there quicker on Saturday they're going to effing well kick the shit out of you, I'm telling you.'

It lasted an hour but must have seemed like four. Butler and his colleagues in the Welsh squad for Saturday's international were excused Prosser's final thirty minutes. They groped their way inside, glazed of eye. In twenty minutes the young captain had emerged, glowing with health, showered and changed into sports jacket, collar and tie. 'Hey, what's this, Ed, the back-to-England look?'

It was back indeed to his other world and his wife, back across the Wye and the Severn to where, comparatively, unemployment figures are still just a statistic on a schoolmaster's blackboard. Around Pontypool the state of the nation is grim, the dole queues dreadfully long.

We speed away. Up there on the hill above the sleepy, hybrid border town of Monmouth is Butler's old school. It is many years since the Welsh XV was captained by a former public schoolboy. This new Welsh captain is a throwback to the days of Gents and Players. For that reason one or two Welshmen this afternoon are saying they would get a buzz out of Butler – an Oxbridge boy to boot – personally falling flat on his face next Saturday afternoon. He is a first generation public schoolboy and a first generation Welshman. His grandfather was a brickie in the Scunthorpe steelworks. His grammar-school father became a research chemist and moved south where he played amateur soccer for Wycombe Wanderers and three times for English representative XIs as an inside forward. Eddie's mother is a Londoner who at the time her husband took up a job in South Wales was loathe to go west. She is now passionate about Wales, as is the boy's soccer-playing father about rugby union. They run a guesthouse in Raglan.

Monmouth School, with disdain, would not allow its boys to be selected for Welsh schools' sides. When he left Eddie traditionally walked the Jarrett way to attend a trial with Newport. 'How many Welsh schoolboy caps have you?' he was asked. 'None, sir.' 'Well, go and stand over on that pitch with those others and I'll try and have a look at you later,' said the coach. And that was that. He went to Cambridge to read languages, impressed in the trials and won a blue the following year as a tearaway forward. Back home the previous summer, during a game of cricket, a friend suggested he join the more 'villagey' Pontypool RFC. At once Pross sensed a prospect, and soon the gauche and gangly Cambridge blue was packing down in his vacations alongside the redoubtable Terry Cobner, then Jeff Squire, and even behind the famed front row itself. Every match was a senior tutorial. 'Up and Under, Here We Go . . .' as Max Boyce's famous chorus celebration of Pontypool's great trio, Faulkner, Windsor and Price goes – the Viet Gwent!

Ideally Butler could do with another inch or two to make his line-out play even better, and he admits he's not an Allan Wells from the blocks, but he has a sturdy, relentless, Pontypool stamina for cornerflagging and a beady eye for the right place at the right time. West Walians, with their more romantic nature, feel Butler lacks the presence and charisma to be an international middle-of-the-back. But Prosser's more pragmatic theories hold that a good forward is seldom noticed as an individual; he must be deep in the thick of things, and one has to regard the entity of eight men playing as one unit. Keep your eye on Butler and you will see that he never, ever, stops working, beavering, burrowing, tidying, cajoling.

In 1979 Carwyn James was publicly canvassing for Butler to be made captain of the Welsh B side. 'The playing of Butler will reap dividends in two or three years . . . his Pontypool forward unit is the most formidable of any club side in the world; it has physical presence [and] drill of the most sophisticated nature which just goes rolling and rolling along in front of its large and critical audience at Pontypool Park.' Not to mention the dogs.

Butler played his first senior game for Wales in 1980. After the arrogant, sing-song exuberance of the decade of the dragon, the results of the eighties have been near-humiliating for Wales, and this means that this honest, open-faced, humorous athlete has a job on his hands. His hair is already flecked with grey.

His priority on Saturday against England, in concert with Terry Holmes, will be to lock in the strengths of his back row around the skirts of the scrummage. He must control the passions and then release them. No. 8, of course, was the position of Mervyn Davies, one of Wales's most legendary captains. That is an added spur, especially as the old warrior said in the *Daily Mirror* last week that he did not think Butler worth his place.

You fear for young Eddie Butler. He has been set a formidably difficult examination. For over a decade Welsh rugby wallowed in unprecedented success. They won everything in sight and with such power, such *presumption* that when the fall came a year ago the clatter of falling egos and expectation was grievous to behold. Last season Wales were left with the Championship's Wooden Spoon. Total humiliation which was gleefully italicised by the Scots running riot in the final match on Wales's own high altar at the Arms Park. For nine months the Welsh have found a comfort only in their own melancholy. A black-dog gloom pervades every

'What's this, Ed – the back-to-England look?' Four times each week Gent becomes Player when Butler leaves the Cotswold cloisters of Cheltenham for the fraught, rumbustious, business of shielding scrum-halves for Pontypool or Wales. Here in Paris Butler guards Holmes (on knees), and blocks Imbernon as he makes a lunge for Perkins. James holds the fort at the front and Dospital, Dintrans and Joinel can only peek over the parapet.

dingy bar and working men's club. The Principality is shrouded in pessimism. Their new team cannot play. 'Oo's this bloody Brit, Butler, anyway?'

But the fall *had* to be a spectacular one – for the heights the previous decade had scaled had been unprecedented. Sometimes, indeed, their play and their players were out of sight. As Butler drove me back to Cheltenham, I closed my eyes – and a million images spool through the memory . . .

Over a dozen years it lasted. At the end of the 1966 season the Welsh RFU took the unprecedented decision to appoint a national team coach, but I like to think the whole barnstorm started a wet midwinter Sunday morning of the same year, when a nervous trainee teacher called Edwards presented himself at Trinity College, Carmarthen, for a private practice with his new Welsh trials partner called John. Edwards had a swank tracksuit and shiny boots; John had a hangover and plimsolls; rain bucketed down on the Ystrad playing fields at Johnstown. It was an unlikely setting for the immortal exchange, as famous in the Welsh Dictionary of Quotations as 'No room at the inn' . . .

'Look, Gareth, you throw 'em and I'll catch 'em. Let's leave it at that and piss off home.'

'Don't worry about my passes, boy. I can sling 'em from anywhere. Just make sure you catch 'em, that's all.'

A year later a junior selector at the London Welsh club in London suggested promoting a 3rd XV No. 8 who 'is not much good as a player, but he's tall and might win us a bit of ball at the back of the line-out.' Six matches later Mervyn Davies won his first cap for Wales. And then came Max Boyce, live at Treorchy, singing his hymns and arias, 'Land of My Fathers', 'Ar Hyd y nos', and so began the most celebrated episode in a century of international rugby football.

The scripture that took shape was to have Barry John see Woolworths' girls curtsy to him and mothers bring babes to touch the hem of his Levis. While I, a dozen years later, was to sit in a dingy Fishguard taproom and half-hear on the radio that the new pope from Poland had decided against a posh St Peter's coronation. He would not be wearing the priceless Triple Crown of all the pontiffs in history. At which the little drinker next to me murmured: 'Triple Crown? I s'pose Gareth wouldn't give him a borrow of it, see.'

As the new faith blazed across the little land it lit up in flames the names of other major apostles to follow Mervyn the Swervin', who was nearly a martyr for the cause; of Benny, whose three shy sidesteps, legs working like barbers' scissors, had set up the greatest try in history; of Gerald, frail and lonely on his touchline, warming his hands in his armpits and with his shirt buttoned up to the neck, who could suddenly pin his ears back and go like an electric hare. And last to go was Japes . . . I'm not sure that of all those scarlet pimpernels J.P.R. was not the most original and breathtaking of the lot. His ability to turn defensive indestructibility into heroic counter-attack is the definitive stuff of sport.

On the morning of the Welsh trial one year J.P.R.'s Ford Capri crashed into a tanker in a narrow lane near Llansannor. He was shaken but, of course, he still turned out that afternoon. It inspired a Welsh poet, Tom Bellion, to write a piece entitled 'J.P.R. collides with tanker – the tanker spent a comfortable night in hospital but is expected to recover.' Exactly.

There were those passionate pep talks by Clive Rowlands, former captain, and the coach and the topcat. Fifteen times he would bark out, 'What are you going to do?' Each time he would point at a player, who would bellow back 'WIN!' (Though when John Lloyd of Bridgend used to play he was always allowed to reply, 'EAT 'EM!') Then the monologue would start: 'You are going out to win for your country! For Wales! For your Dada! For the Mam who nursed you! For your village! For your school! For your pit! For your works! For your wife! For your sweetheart! For your auntie Gladwys! For that tart you met on Saturday! For the man on the bus this morning!' (One time a new cap had been playing hard for twenty minutes when, in a lull, he said to his colleague in the scrum – 'Hey, wait a mo': I haven't got an Auntie Gladwys. And that tart on Saturday said she didn't want to see me again!')

No pep-talk passion, to my mind, could match the one of that most Welsh of Welshmen, Ray Gravell. They were all steamed up and ready to clatter out and take on twenty English bulldozers, if need be, when Gravell called them back. The tears rolled down into his sandy beard: 'Boys! Boys! Just a mo', I've got a telegram here I want to read to you: "Best wishes to my son", it says, boys. "All my love" . . . and do you know who signed it? "Best wishes from Mam and Shamrock". *Chi'n gwbod pwy yw Shamrock bois? Y gath!* Do you know who Shamrock is, boys? The effin' cat! The effin' cat sent us a telegram!'

Feed me till I want no more, indeed. The memories spool on . . . sitting in a London bar on the eve of a Cardiff match where, over champagne, John Morgan, handsome, moneyed Dai-the-Box, publicly reckoned his Welsh XV were getting too big for their Adidas boots. At which his pal, Alan Watkins, admitted: 'We have become a mechanised team, boy. We Welsh are to rugby football what Alf Ramsey's England were to soccer. Stereotyped. A machine. We might win everything, but it would do us good to lose. For the good of the game.'

And as the list of honours rolled on the supporters demanded more, ever more. Once, said Mervyn Davies, then captain, they would be happy for the Welsh team just to win by a single point – 'they're spoilt now. They come up to you and say, "Why didn't you win by more?" It has begun to get to the players. After the England game we came off the field as if we'd been beaten. We'd won by a record number of points on English soil, but we sat in the changing room as if we'd lost because we'd only scored twenty-one points instead of thirty or more!'

The arrogance, the one-eyed insularity – and the cocky wit too – was never more in evidence than one horrendous Sunday morning in the Orly airport lounge in January 1975, the day after Wales had walloped France by more than twenty points. The charter flights were about to board when the bleary queues were ripped apart by a group of Black September terrorists spraying everything in sight with machine gun bullets. Hundreds dived for cover, the fearful attack moved on – and then the momentary, eerie silence was broken when, from under a table and waving a red and white scarf, in lilting Celtic sing-song came the plea – 'Don't take your beating to heart so, Froggies; it's only a game at the end of the day, isn't it?'

Occasionally, just occasionally, they lost. Or rather, the other side scored more points. England last beat them at Cardiff in 1963 by 13–6. That was a frosty, bitter, ear-biting day and the pitch was like the main arena at the Silver Blades. It was one of the last of the haughty public school English sides, and they got the Scarlets in an awful flather by laughing at their being issued with flannel vests to wear under their shirts. Come to think of it, England have won on their home patch at

Twickenham only twice against Wales in a quarter of a century – and that's counting 1974, when an Irish referee disallowed two Welsh tries and the Whites won 16–12. Max Boyce declares still that his charity concert royalties go not to refugees, but to a little house in Ireland that stands beneath the trees – 'the Sunshine Home near Dublin for blind Irish referees'.

Following that 1974 game Mervyn Davies explained baldly: 'There is no reason a Welsh XV should ever be beaten by England unless we come up against indifferent refereeing.' When England won in 1980 it was because a Welshman, Ringer, was sent off – by an Irish referee. Even the result of the very first match between the two countries, which England won 69–0 on Mr Richardson's Field at Blackheath in 1881, is explained away by a parenthesis in the official history of the Welsh Rugby Union – 'the match was umpired by A. Guillemard, of Kent, who was the president of the English RU.' Those, of course, were the days before neutral officials.

A few winters ago I was present at a wailing Welsh wake in the press box at Cardiff when the All Blacks beat Wales with a disputed penalty in the very last minute of injury time – a penalty awarded by an English referee, Roger Quittenton, for an infringement by the Welsh lock, Wheel – at exactly the moment his Kiwi opposite number, Haden, dramatically 'fell' out of the line-out as, on his own admission, a ploy to con the referee. Quittenton insisted he had penalised Wheel and had not even seen Haden's sly antics. The Welsh still find it hard to swallow. They were in the lead by one point and were singing home the boys – then McKecknie kicked the goal, they were two points adrift, and Quittenton blew the whistle. Up in the press box – where the legendary Taffia, one by one, had completed active service and to a man had taken up the pen – calamity! It was like gate-crashing the Cosa Nostra's back parlour the day Grandpa died.

'Don't talk to me yet,' said Mervyn Davies to his Fleet Street ghost-writer. 'We've never had to compose an obituary before.' 'That result,' said Barry John, 'came from Hollywood tactics by New Zealand: the bastards simply conned the ref.'

However, New Zealand was one thing – even though that match was dolled up, to be for the World Championship. No; in the long-time logic of denied nationhood and the fervour of a new religion with a grip more strong than that of the declining Bethesda chapels that was nothing when compared with the Ultimate Championship – the eighty-minute annual against England. 'Losing to the English is simply unthinkable,' says Gareth. 'We are warriors,' says Barry, 'out to get revenge for hurts by Saxons of centuries ago.' A Welshman's nightly prayer, says Mervyn, is 'Lord, if we've got to get beat, let it not be by England.'

As part of their determination to give back the Wooden Spoon the Welsh RU have called in a group of dietary boffins to advise on menus. This week the squad have been surreptitiously consulting their diet sheets – great big hairy men pretending to be Jane Fondas and Green

Goddesses. High protein – meat, fish, and cheese – till Wednesday then, as a last blast till the day itself, carbohydrates – pastas and mountains of mashed potatoes. The marathon runner knows it well. Immediately before the match they will have toast and jam with – to get the adrenalin going – two mugs of black coffee. Caffeine mobilises the body fats, they say.

Dutifully, Eddie Butler has not cried *basta* on the *pasta* – 'though nobody's getting me off my All-Bran: must have my daily roughage.' Once upon a time the Welsh dressing room was littered with tubes of glucose tablets: the boffins have banned them – 'just put sugar in the bloodstream, totally useless, purely psychological.' Now the players are on selected vitamin pills – 'sweating makes you lose vital vitamins contained in body liquids.' Not like a sportsman in the old days when the match-day diet would become – like, say, putting on your left sock first – an unbreakable ritual and superstition. Brian Thomas, the mighty Neath second row, would touch nothing but a pound of grapes for breakfast: he'd devour them through the morning like a Roman emperor. Mervyn Davies would order a whacking great fry-up for 10 a.m. – sausages, tomatoes, fried potatoes, lashings of fried bread, the lot – then have a piece of fish and a cup of tea for his lunch at one o'clock! Dr J.P.R., as you would expect, would eat nothing all day but a couple of slices of toast and honey – though Max Wiltshire, the Aberavon lock, wouldn't consider playing unless he had his curry and rice; he'd carry around his little packets of Vesta in case it wasn't on the menu.

The one-and-only Ray Gravell, of course, ate soft centres. Some players – the incomparable Dai Watkins, for one – would eat nothing at all on the day of a match, and nor would the muscle-packed Pontypool front-row. Years ago their mentor, Prosser, pronounced, 'Give a lion a meal and he'll go to sleep. Keep him hungry and he'll go hunting all day.' Thus, while their international team-mates of the old days were wolfing down their pre-match steaks, their fry-ups, their grapes or their curries, the Ponty's front-row would dutifully wrap their entrecôtes in serviettes, to eat them cold when the match was over.

Just one of the legendary Pontypool front row remains in the Welsh side – Graham Price, who in the game against England will become the most capped forward in Welsh history. 'Did you see Pricey go tonight?' asks Butler. I did. 'It's a myth that he's just a fantastically hard scrumma-ger. He's surprisingly light on his feet and very fast for a prop. He's always *there*. You watch him on Saturday.'

We were into Gloucestershire. Wasn't it too much of a culture jump? I asked at last. 'No, I never really think about it. I love Pontypool, and ever since Day One everyone's been very good to me and just treated me as one of the boys, whether it be Pross or the players or the committee. Anyway, quite honestly I'm a little left-wing in my views so I don't feel different to the others. And I'm not different – in any way.' What about the jump between coaching English public schoolboys and being coached at a top-level Welsh 'industrial' club? 'Not a ha'porth of difference. I approach coaching the boys in the same way as I approach my own rugby: the basis simply being to play as well as I can – and as they can. No one can do fairer than that. The boys at Cheltenham train four days a week and get much enjoyment from it and we mould them into a team in just the way we would at Pontypool.'

Butler might like coaching and playing rugby, but to watch he'd prefer a top-class soccer match. Though he admits to an admiration of extroverts such as Brian Clough and Dennis Lillee (and, obviously, dear old Pross) he is not a tub-thumping captain. No fire and brimstone dressing-room speeches from him – 'some I've heard make me want to snigger they're so embarrassing.' Organisation, he says, is almost the whole battle – 'Real captaincy should be done before the team takes the field. Naturally you have to make decisions on penalties and so on during the match but the basic work has been done long before. Motivation? If playing for Wales in itself is not sufficient motivation what is? If you gee everyone up too much you can all lose perspective. You can go into a game over-motivated and freeze when you're on the pitch. That has even happened at Pontypool. I don't go along with too much chanting and stamping: at this level the match and the atmosphere and the red shirt should be almost enough.'

The next day he was teaching again. Then at teatime this self-same journey, but further west, to Bridgend where his brand-new Welsh team were congregating for practice. Two days later, in the early afternoon of Saturday, they will have their final coffee at the Angel Hotel and then Eddie Butler, erect, nervous, proud, will lead his apprehensive young men, as his predecessors have for a century, through the frenzied, jostling crowds to the national cauldron. *'Pob lwc heddi!'* 'Good luck, boys! For Wales, boys!'

A hundred and seven years ago the Cheltenham College Rules, at twenty players a side, provided the code for the very first organised club games to be played, first at Cardiff, then Merthyr, then Pontypool. Through Eddie Butler, new captain of Wales, strands and spirits across a century of seasons come together on Saturday afternoon. What the English public schoolboys of Cheltenham long ago gave to Wales, in a way Pontypool will be giving back. With a vengeance, mind.

CHAPTER SEVEN

The Chattanooga Choo-choo

In the week before a previous Wales v England game a small ad had appeared in the *South Wales Echo*: 'DESPERATELY WANTED – Ticket for Match. Offer Rolls Royce Car In Exchange'. Next day there was a reply: 'Will Yesterday's Advertiser Please State What Year Is Rolls Royce.' Just before the game Gareth Edwards was summoned to Buckingham Palace to receive his MBE. There was a cartoon in the *Echo* by Gren Jones, the Max Boyce of pen and ink, showing two pithead workers reading the headline, 'QUEEN SEES GARETH AT PALACE'. The caption read: 'Amazing the lengths some people go to, to try and get a ticket.'

This year tickets can never have been in shorter supply. The Arms Park is being rebuilt: the whole of the south side is under construction. By next year the stadium will be a vast concrete horseshoe, with only one remaining end terrace hinting at what the old place used to be like. Everyone was here – even the man from *New Society*. It was more than a rugby match, he said: Wales versus England was a clash of class, culture and temperament. The Arms Park had 'gone secular', he went on, now that the ancient, pitched 'Methodist chapel' stands had been replaced by a high-tech bowl.

In the evening the Welsh team, as is their custom, went to the cinema then to bed early at the Angel Hotel, just across the road from the stadium. The English side stayed up later in their modern hotel off the motorway on the Severn Bridge side of the city. A few watched television, while others chatted in threes and fours in the lounge before drifting off to bed in ones and twos.

In spite of their defeat by France, England would start the game as favourites. The centre, Woodward, was still unfit – Davies retaining his place – but, more crucially, Wheeler's injured ankle had not improved and so Steve Mills, a Cirencester stalwart, was brought in as hooker. This, hearteningly, brought the Gloucester representation to two, for the badly injured Colclough had been replaced at lock by Steve Boyle, who had once been a reserve soccer goalkeeper for Gloucester City. He was brought up in Lancashire but in his last year at school his family moved to the south-west. When he was eighteen and in his first job in a bank, he met two friends in a pub. 'They said they were a man short for their rugby match. I had nothing to do so I went along. I didn't think much of the game but I had a whale of a time with the rest of them afterwards. I thought: "This is a better laugh than football. I'll give it a go." ' Eleven years later – and now over eighteen stone – his name would be indelibly writ on the roll-call of one of sport's most famous fixtures.

As England's former captain, Beaumont, remarked in the bar on the eve of this latest encounter – 'When you play Wales at Cardiff you are not just up against fifteen fellows in red shirts, you are up against a whole nation.' Indeed, it might literally have seemed like that sometimes since England's last victory here – on the ice in 1963. In the nine matches between the two sides in Cardiff since then, Wales have run in 207 points to England's measly 83, with a run-away try ratio of 32 to 6. When you reflect on that record you realise why the telephone rang for Steve Smith in the hotel just now. It was his old friend and Sale clubmate, Fran Cotton. Said Fran, 'I played in Wales for England five times. We never won once. With Sale I never won away against a Welsh club. You've just got to do it for me tomorrow, kid.' 'Don't worry, Fran lad,' said the captain of England. 'We'll do the business for you, have no fear.'

The fortune tellers and soothsayers of Fleet Street were examining the entrails in the small print of the *Rothmans Rugby Yearbook*. When England won in 1963, much against the odds, they had taken a gamble beforehand and chosen a new captain, Sharp, and six uncapped young players, including Davis, the present England coach. This time it was the Welsh who had picked five new caps to play under a new captain in Butler. That's the sort of 'coincidence' we hacks like. Also, exactly fifty years ago the Welsh had come up with one of their most spectacular victories of the whole series when they chose seven new players – including the Rydal schoolboy, Wilf Wooller – and won 7–3, their first-ever victory at Twickenham in ten attempts. And on and on we rabitted into the night . . . while the young men slept. Or, in the case of England's two Gloucester men, and Wales' five debutants probably didn't.

One, or even two, of these five may have the multitude composing songs by teatime tomorrow. Over the years Wales have made a habit of picking first-match prodigies: Lewis Jones and Keith Jarrett come to mind. Might tomorrow be the day of all his days for Mark Wyatt, full-back and student of both mining and philosophy; or for Malcolm Dacey, a carpenter and latest in the line from the fly-half factory; or David Pickering, flanker and architectural assistant; or Mark Ring, centre and, at twenty, the youngest man on the field? When he heard he was playing Ring had burst into uncontrollable tears. As Barry John said to me once, 'You've no idea what that shirt, that red, scarlet, priceless shirt means: it's like getting an Emmy, a Tony, an Oscar, a Nobel prize – you name it, that's it. And it means too that wherever you go, to Fylde or Fiji or New Zealand, or up the road to Tumble, you'll open the programme and there'll be your name, and after it there'll be an asterisk. Just a little asterisk, but it will mean the world, it will mean "Welsh international".'

Barry John in fact bridged the gap. Things had changed since his first cap, against Australia in 1966. Now it was squad weekends and tactics and fancy tracksuits. Before the coaches were appointed – Wales led the way in 1967 – players would turn up on the day with their kit in an attaché case, or an army rucksack even. I remember Clem Thomas telling me once how he travelled to Cardiff on the morning of an international – I'm not sure if it wasn't the day of his famous cross-kick in 1953, a last-minute stroke of inspiration when he was hemmed in on the south touchline; he punted the ball towards the posts and Ken Jones gathered to score. Pandemonium! Anyway, Clem was sitting in the railway carriage coming up for the match from Swansea. His neighbours were naturally talking about the game. One man was boasting about his true and certain friendship with Clem. Our hero kept mum. When the train arrived at the city, Clem reached to the luggage rack for his bag, on which were tied his boots. What, said one of his fellow travellers, not going to watch the match then? 'No,' said Clem, 'I'm playing in it, actually.' What's your name? asked the 'true, dear friend of Clem'. 'As it happens, it's Thomas, I'm afraid,' said Clem.

Two of the new Welsh caps in that famous victory of England's in 1963 were the Dais – Watkins at fly-half and Hayward at wing-forward. They nearly didn't make it. Hayward promised to give Watkins a lift to Cardiff on the morning of the match in his Hillman: he lived even further up the Western Valley, at Blaina. Recalls Hayward: 'It is so cold up there that the locals organise sunshine tours to Lapland, and the daffodils need lagging. Since Dai was misguided enough to play for Newport it was assumed that he wouldn't know the way to Cardiff, and I was delegated to pick him up in my car. (No overnight stays in luxury hotels in those days; it was a journey into the unknown in my clapped-out Husky or a 2s 6d return on a Ralphs bus. Either option offered about the same chance of survival.) After a journey during which I saw more ice than Captain Scott I arrived in Blaina to find that Dai had been taken out by the Arctic Platoon of Special Air Service. My resentment of this had a profound bearing in the outcome of the match.' Hayward just made it in time, looking, Watkins recalls, 'white about the gills'. The darting, little fly-half had, in fact, hitched a lift with an intrepid van-load of supporters, thinking Hayward had either got stuck in a snow drift, or just forgotten.

Now we were almost ready. The English players dribbed and drabbed down to the dining room for breakfast. In the city centre, at the Angel, the Welsh team's physiotherapist and general factotum had gone along the corridor, waking each player at nine o'clock. This was Gerry Lewis's 99th match in the service of Wales. Knock, knock. 'Mornin', boys. Sleep well?' . . . He opens the curtains. 'Not a bad day. No rain at least. Might be a handling game, eh? Anyway, lads, team talk 11.30 – okay? . . .' And off he goes to the next room to repeat the same spiel – what's 99 times 15?

The Chattanooga Choo-choo

John Taylor, now a journalist but not many years before the bearded, barnstorming flanker with a pruning-shears tackle, once described Lewis: 'Gerry is a living legend for the Welsh team and nobody can really imagine an international weekend without him. His most important function is team physiotherapist and there are very few players who do not owe one or two of their caps to him. He took over the job from his father in 1962 and has worked miracles with his massage and medication ever since. Apart from that he organises the weekend, doing everything from looking after the kit to ordering the theatre tickets. But first thing in the morning, around nine o'clock, he is nothing short of a nuisance. However badly any player has slept they all agree that for some reason they are asleep at the time Gerry calls. Sometimes Gerry deigns to knock but if he is really working well he has persuaded the hotel management to give him a pass key. Whatever happens, he will not go away, the door has to be opened and he is so cheerful it makes you sick. In five minutes everyone has had an enquiry into their health, a weather report, the latest on a player with a slight twinge, the routine programme for the day, the latest news, apart from the match, and the latest in his never-ending supply of stories.'

Outside the Angel the crowds were gathering. The tickets were really in short supply. 'Forty quid for a two-fifty enclosure!' said someone. 'Scandal, it is. A scandal.' But he and his friend were fingering their back-pocket fivers. It's either furtive whispers or shouting. Some carried placards – 'I'm not greedy – I only want one ticket!' Another says, 'My mam will kill me if I don't get her a ticket.'

The *Western Mail* has an eight-page special. *The Times* has two articles to get us in the mood, one by Alan Watkins, the political writer, in reminiscent vein: 'There was no television in those days. If you wanted to see the international you had to go there. For the England and Wales match, as for all internationals, my father always wore his best suit. He also wore a hat, a heavy overcoat, leather gloves and, depending on the weather, a silk or woollen scarf. Though he was by no means sympathetic to communism – quite the reverse – the general effect of his outfit was to make him resemble a large but politically obscure member of the Politburo who was about to take the salute at a parade of tanks.

'In fact he was a Welsh schoolmaster who, while neither vain nor pushful, felt he had standards to maintain. He would no more have gone to the match with a leek and a red-and-white scarf than he would have appeared in front of his class with a false nose. I was expected to be correctly attired likewise, even if less splendidly.

'The first match we saw together was not, strictly speaking, an international. It was the "Victory International" of 1946 for which no full caps were awarded. We travelled from Carmarthenshire to Cardiff in a hired single-decker bus (there were few coaches then). Also on the bus was another son of the village, Hugh Lloyd-Davies, in his pilot officer's uniform, who was playing for Wales at full-back.'

The other article was an interview with Ronnie Boon, who scored all the seven points that defeated England exactly half a century ago. With minutes to go Wales were leading by just 4–3 when the English dasher, Elliott, broke clear away from the halfway line. He had no one to beat. Wales were surely done for. 'Imagine the scene. The stands full of Englishmen on their feet cheering madly, and the banks behind the posts lined with stunned Welshmen seeing a great victory about to slip away from them. Elliott would have touched down under the crossbar. Then Wilf Wooller, in his first international, a tall, young man with his long sprinter's strides, imperceptibly at first, and then noticeably and with increasing velocity, closed the gap and brought Elliott crashing down near the Welsh line. Wilf undoubtedly saved the game for us.

'Wales were still hanging on to their one-point lead. Harry Bocott nearly made it eight points for Wales but his drop kick hit an upright. [A drop goal was worth four points then.] The forwards, playing a tight, destroying game, carried play into the English half. A scrum formed, there was a quick heel and Harry Bocott feinted to the open side. Maurice Turnbull served Claude Davey cleanly who came blind side and made ground brilliantly. Aarvold the England captain had to go for Claude. I took Claude's pass and Brown the full-back could not come round in time to stop me touching down. It was a piece of cake.'

Ronnie Boon, seventy-three now but apparently looking twenty years younger, also recalled: 'Fifteen minutes before the game was due to start Walter Rees, secretary of the Welsh Rugby Union and a great and dominant character in Welsh rugby, came into the dressing room and said: "Now boys, I want you to remember this. I don't want to see you charging for taxis to Cardiff when you put your expenses in." Wages were low and there was a lot of unemployment in those days. For the boys who worked in industry, charging taxi fares when they had taken buses to Cardiff from their homes was the only way they could make half-a-crown or so to help their families and give them an extra pint or two. Who could blame them? I still smile when I think of Walter, worrying about expenses at such a moment.'

Now, exactly fifty years on, their successors arrived, the Welsh team walking through the throng outside the Angel. England purred through the crowd in a snazzy coach. They inspected the pitch in their civvies, hands in pockets and pretending to look nonchalant. As Beaumont said the previous night, it was 'pretty awesome for an Englishman to play at Cardiff'. Some forty years ago Wing-Cmdr Cyril Gadney, the referee, in the last minute of an international penalised an Englishman for lying on the ball. No matter that he was unconscious! Wales kicked the winning goal – and Gadders said afterwards: 'It was a horrible thing to have to do to an Englishman: it was as bad as taking a man's life.' A quarter of a century ago David Marques, an elongated Oxbridge line-out jumper, was scraped from the Cardiff mud, having been in turn gouged, kicked, raked

and punched by two coalface toughs and two iron-mittened steelwor-
kers. He immediately shook hands with each of his assailants. 'Why do
that? They tried to kill you,' said a colleague. 'I want them to feel proper
cads,' replied Master Marques.

Not so long ago, in that same dressing room where the team were
changing now, an English captain, who was something in the City of
London, offered a pep-talk to his lilywhites. 'Look, chaps, I'm damn
nervous too . . . anyone got a fag before we go out?' – which he followed,
once out, by winning the toss but then, nerves still a-jangle, giving the
Welsh captain choice of ends *as well as* kick-off.

Gareth Edwards once told how the Welsh in the next cabin (the teams
had adjoining, temporary changing rooms while they were rebuilding
another part of the Arms Park) split their sides when they heard the
England RFU president go into the England changing room just before
kick-off and announce, 'Stand to, chaps, my wife would like a word with
you' – and to be sure, the jock-strapped army stood to attention with their
Vaselined thighs and cauliflower ears to hear the voice of Thatcherite-
blue exhort them, 'just go out and do jolly, jolly well!'

Outside, the ticketless multitude stood quiet, in limbo. Inside there was
silence, then a collective murmur, a rumble of expectation as Smith led
England out. Next, silence again for a moment – then tumult and, at the
solitary terrace end, an excited flutter of flags and banners and scarves.
Red was the colour. They sang the National Anthem and 'Land of My
Fathers', the sound of it bouncing around Mr Wimpey's girders and the
concrete blocks on his building site where the South Stand was and will
be.

Alas, in the event, all the expectations, all the anticipation, seemed to
waft pungently around those cranes and girders and then, as soon as they
kicked off, float up and away from the Arms Park itself. At any rate, it was
a woefully disappointing match, a 13–13 draw. Neither side deserved to
win. England had the better of the first half; Wales finished the stronger
and, indeed, Holmes might have won it for them when he launched
himself at the English line in the final minute and could only have been
stopped an inch or so away. England's Championship debutants, Mills
and Boyle, acquitted themselves well enough, as did Wyatt and James for
Wales. Generally, everyone was sucked into the tedium and tension of it.
I cannot remember being so disappointed at a major sporting extravaganza. Often the atmosphere and throbbing drama of the big occasion carries
you through the hour or so. Not here.

The one brief passage of quality was England's try. From a scrum
around halfway and some twenty metres in from the Committee Box
touchline Smith fed Cusworth, who ran diagonally at the Welsh centre,
Ring. Dodge, England's inside centre, crissed as Cusworth crossed, in a
perfect dummy scissors, to allow the Leicester fly-half a moment to
consider his pass to his clubmate, Hare, who was pelting straight and true
from behind. It was a beautifully timed pass. Hare had raised quite a

The artist checks his perspectives . . . Hare wills his record-breaking kick in off the post at Cardiff.

The Chattanooga Choo-choo. All stations from Leicester: Dodge has crissed as Cusworth has crossed – and Hare rattles through like a train, with Carleton outside him. Wales are on their heels and the England winger (OPPOSITE) supplies the dramatic finishing touch.

gallop; he breached the defence and only had to draw Wyatt before handing the thing, gift-wrapped, to Carleton, who sped over the line flamboyantly. It was a Leicester move – they call it 'the Chattanooga', apparently, for Hare has to be going like a choo-choo train when he receives the ball. He was. Nothing could be finer. It provided England with a 7–6 half-time lead – Wyatt having kicked a penalty and Dacey dropped a goal to match Hare's early penalty. In the second half Smith bravely threw out a difficult, bellyflop pass to allow Cusworth to drop a goal to put England further ahead. But first a penalty by Wyatt and then a disputed, scrambling try by Squire with thirteen minutes left made Wales, briefly, look like winning. But the steady, resourceful, impressive Hare equalised with a penalty – which, incidentally, broke England's points-scoring record of 138 set by Bob Hiller just over a decade ago.

At the end there was little of the usual joyous jig of kids running on to the field. It had been an awfully limp afternoon. But then the whole weekend was an anti-climax. The traditional jingle-jangle atmosphere was muted. Cricketing, I have missed the Arms Park for three winters, during which time the Welsh XV has fallen on hard times, but even the Arms Park choral society seems a thing of the glorious past. Patchy stuff today, unharmonious and overstrained. Could it be the ambience has been irretrievably ruined by the swank of the new stadium?

Or is it because the traditional hardcore supporters are now left outside in their donkey jackets pleading for tickets, and the middle-class debenture-holders need take their posh post-prandial seats only a few minutes before the kick-off? In the morning, John Williams, who has conducted the celebrated St Albans band for many years, admitted: 'In the old days all the people in the stand had been brought up in the chapel tradition and they could sing off twenty hymns without any problem. Nearly everybody in the ground could sing non-stop for at least three-quarters of an hour . . . Now they don't have the same religious training, and with modern music and pop songs they only remember the choruses.'

On Saturday, just before the teams came out, they were playing 'John Brown's Body' – not quite the thing as years gone by.

With Wales mouldering so, England could and should have walked it. They might not get such a chance again for another twenty years. They must be kicking themselves – though, Hare apart, most of them would have missed. What are Wales going to do when they play France in six weeks? Without taking a kick at goal, the dusky Blanco could beat them on his own. What, indeed, are Wales going to do in a fortnight against Scotland?

At the end, both captains, Smith and Butler, admitted the possibility that their sides had contributed to a stinker. Always, however, smiles are not far from their lips. As he clumped down the tunnel, disappointed and nursing injured ribs, Smith mimed to me a soccer *Match of the Day* quote – 'Well, David, a point away from home; the manager and the lads are very pleased.'

Butler talked us through Squire's questionable, scrabbling, untidy try: 'Magic! There was a bobbing ball, a pounce, a shove, a scream of joy; I didn't see a thing, mind you, but I can definitely tell you it was a move that we've been working on.'

After the conference I commiserated my cheerios to Butler, ending: 'See you at Murrayfield.' He drew a hand across his throat. 'Blimey, I don't know if I'll be going up there yet.'

And indeed, there might be quite a bit of blood around when the English and Welsh selectors get a grip on throats these next days.

Nevertheless, the Welsh seemed far happier than the English. Although the game ended with a siege on the England line, by then Wales should have been well behind. Within half an hour of the game, as we waited in the damp, concrete stadium vaults for the post-match press conference, none of us could recall even one spirit-stirring passage from the game apart from England's try. The stalemate, on reflection, was justice. 'I hear the replay will be on Wednesday,' remarked the former Cardiff international, Keith Rowlands, as he passed by, adding, 'but I will not be attending.' On the other hand, his namesake, Clive, the chairman of selectors, was not abashed. 'Our rucking was magnificent,' he said. 'We have the makings of a team.' For England, Rogers and Davis attended. I thought it ominous that Smith was not there – he was having his ribs looked at, said Rogers – especially when the chairman of selectors said pointedly, 'We should have had the game well sewn up by half-time, but we did not make the right decisions at half-back.'

In the corridor, Willie-John McBride, with an altogether more difficult selection job to do inside two months, leaned on a wall. He looked as though he now realised the difficulty of his Lions' brief. The brogue was soft as he searched for some brightness. Well, Holmes, he said, was Holmes – 'and Hare got England out of trouble whenever their mistakes played them into it'. There was not much else to cheer him on his way back to Ulster.

The anti-climax of the day had me almost relieved to be driving back eastwards across the Severn Bridge. On the car radio, all the pundits agreed in their post mortems, though Clive Rowlands was still cockily asserting that 'at least, next time they come here, it will be twenty-two years since England beat us at Cardiff.' And, perhaps thinking it had been jaded me, not jaded them, that had caused me to lament so over the once-celebrated singing of the Arms Park congregation, I was pleased to hear a contributor quoting the journalist, Dai Davies, who had been of the same mind – 'This is a serious matter, my compatriots. If we have to delete *Land of Song* from the tourist brochures what have we Welsh got left but rudimentary cooking and sheep?'

Paris, on the other hand, had staged a good and challenging match in which Scotland had played with keenness, alertness and competitiveness against an initially nervous and uncertain French side, before submitting 15–19. In fact, France did not take the lead until the 37th minute of the second half when, at 15–15, Esteve had spied an opening in the corner and had scored almost before the defenders were twitching in anticipation. And that decisive try, crucially, had come only a handful of minutes after the new Scottish full-back, Dods, had fluffed a straightforward penalty kick from twenty-eight yards. So Scotland were still at it: they had the makings of such a fine side, but as the Scottish reporter in Paris, Ian Archer, put it, 'Like our football people, the rugby men led for long enough but the still silent voice always insisted that they would not be quite good enough to win. And how often has that happened in the past? How aggressively they played, but there was always the certain fragility which we have come to know, and almost love, about the Scots when they put together teams to play sport.'

So all might be decided in Dublin in a fortnight – auld Ireland versus the fizzy frogs. Meanwhile, I would be getting a fuller report in the week when I lunched with an unbiased friend who was nipping over from Paris: Graham Mourie, recently-abdicated king and captain of the world champion All Blacks, is already indelibly writ into history as perhaps the finest of flank-forwards in over a century, as well as one of the game's most serenely strong captains. Unbiased? But how could New Zealanders ever be neutral about European rugby? I wondered who he would mischievously try to 'talk into' the Lions' team.

We lunched at a tiny table in the corner of a fashionable Knightsbridge restaurant. All around, Sloane Rangers whined and vined, squealed and peeled oranges. Graham, hunched and long-legged and unnoticed, munched his salad and his omelette, strained his mineral water through a magnificent walrus moustache, and offered a whispered and concise half-term report on the chances of the British Lions in New Zealand. I had to cup one ear and crane forward to catch his words.

Mourie, the Taranaki farmer of Scots and Italian ancestry, is obviously a gypsy. He corner-flags now round the world. At present he is in Paris – public relations for Pernod. So many receptions, he says, so it is a blessing that the liver virus he caught from his dairy cows makes it, for the time being, against orders to drink alcohol. Yes, another Pernod PRO – Jean-Pierre Rives, perhaps history's *second* best flank-forward and captain – helped him get the job. It is not going to be a lifetime's career, just a fine opportunity to learn French, love France and all that.

Mourie still turns out for fun, for Paris University. He has seen two international matches this season – France against England and Scotland. He is of the mind that the British Lions team could yet be a good one: 'Teams just need one fit specialist – and you must have line-out ball.' Mind, he adds ominously, nearly all the All Blacks we know of and fear will be up for selection. The Scots' match in Paris last week, he reckons, was good, dour, discipline against French flair. 'When I watch a match it's never for enjoyment. I'm not a good critic. I can only play. When I see a good team on the rampage I always think, "What would *I* do to beat them, to disrupt them?" '

Scotland, he thought, have a worthy pack of forwards. They were ahead till almost half-time, but the French flair outside was always going to get a try or two. And so they did. He was delighted at Scotland's back-row forward Leslie. And the scrum-half and captain, 'played splendidly'. 'Laidlaw,' he says, 'must push the Irish scrum-half as deputy to Holmes on the tour.' The rousing Cuthbertson, added Mourie, was a revelation: 'With just an inch or two more line-out height, what a thumping forward he would be!' Then, with ancestral nostalgia: 'They breed them tough and rough and loose up there on the Borders.' Could he be serious about Cuthbertson, I thought? For all his combative barnstorming, the Scot didn't look the most likely line-out Lion to me. Was Mourie being a touch mischievous – tossing in a few names the New Zealanders might be pleased to see on the trip? I was reminded of Don Bradman once 'talking' Malcolm Hilton into the England cricket team – and, once in, murdering him!

From England, Mourie thinks the flanker, Winterbottom, is a must for the Lions. 'He is not all that organised, but he has flair and is fast: that is the beginning of the secret.' The straw-haired Yorkshire rouser has lived and played in New Zealand, so that must help. Jeavons, a 'tight' loose-forward, should also go, although 'he stays close to his pack too much, perhaps.' Mourie reckons the 'much improved' Hare will be the full-back. Of the English backs: 'Well, Slemen is the only man we respect in New Zealand at this stage . . . I suppose Woodward might get the trip.' Poor Slemen, languishing with Liverpool. Nor had Woodward yet turned out for England this season. Indeed, the way things were going for the Lilywhites, might the Lions' chance for those two be improved by absence?

Could it have been Graham's even unconscious 'gamesmanship' that suggested – or rather, just a teeny bit of a hint – that Wheeler might be lucky to make the trip? Or was he trying to 'talk' a feared opponent out of the touring party? 'I suppose Peter,' he admitted, 'must go. But he has to play at the very top of his form; they must decide soon if he is going to be chosen as a hooker first or a captain first. The Irishman and the Scot look pretty good hookers to me.' I felt he wanted Fitzgerald as captain. But was that the unbiased friend talking – or the canny former All Black captain? It was good fun wondering.

How sharp was the rapier of his friend, Rives? Was he in trim for Dublin next week? Would he deal with Campbell? 'I would love to have played against, to have marked Ollie. His kicking is one thing – it could yet win every match for the Lions – but as a first five-eight, look how he commits the flanker to go for him by just holding on to the ball that split-second longer. With the ball in his hands he is a marvellous operator. You see, break-away wing-forward play is actually not necessarily tackling your fly-half, but "shepherding" him, veering him off, making him go the way you want him to.' The finest fly-half Mourie has played against – he missed Barry John by a year or two – is the Argentinian, Porta. 'He could have been the best at any game he chose: at soccer he would have been a World Cup superstar. He has balance and grace and nous. He could transfer the ball in a trice from one hand to the other and he always left a free arm slack so he could "sense" a tackle coming and adjust; he felt the quiver of danger on his shirtsleeve like a cat's whisker. Just phenomenal.' The Argentinian might get away from Rives now. It would be interesting to see if Campbell would. Rives, he thinks, is now playing a tighter, more elderly game: 'He is so much closer these days to his pack; he doesn't range wild and wide to his or to the opposition wingers any more. But his courage, his fearlessness, is still his great and determining attribute.'

That mix of courage and fearlessness and skill and speed and chivalry have ever been Graham Mourie's hallmarks on the playing field. But there is another side too. In the spring of 1981 Mourie announced he would not play against the South African Springboks on the forthcoming tour of New Zealand. The next day, from the pulpit, the Bishop of Auckland, the Reverend Godfrey Wilson, commented on Mourie's statement: 'Suddenly, from the rugby man of the moment, the man at the very peak of his form and fame, comes this quiet, firm voice: "I think there is a moral issue. And it is so important that I cannot play against South Africa." To decide so, that what one believes to be morally right is clearly seen to take precedence over personal ambition and pleasure – that is true leadership.'

After Graham had loped away I washed down all the Perrier with a Cognac. We would meet again in Dublin next week. I raised a glass to that prospect. Also to Master Mourie. In his newly published autobiography, Graham's first chapter quotes Hemingway: 'The great thing is to last and get all your work done and see and hear and learn and understand; and write when there is something that you know; and not before; and not too damned much after . . .'

119

CHAPTER EIGHT

For Ireland, Boys!

Wales went to Murrayfield and I went to Dublin – hesitating briefly about my choice of match, for the Welsh had reconstructed their pack, and the game promised to be one of the most crucial in the whole championship. Butler was still there as captain, but three of the front five who had played against England were dropped: Williams and Moriarty, both of Swansea, were out, but the stunning news was that Graham Price had gone after a run of thirty-nine successive caps in eight years.

Graham was aggrieved. He told the *Daily Mail*'s unrelenting local newshound, Peter Jackson: 'After the service I've given Wales over the years I deserve to be treated a bit better than this.' He went on: 'It takes years to reach your peak as a prop. At thirty-one I feel I'm at my peak. I know there have been problems with the Welsh second-row, but now that the selectors have gone for a second-row combination renowned for their scrummaging and work capacity I thought they'd have given me another chance. I haven't been given an official explanation, but the front five are obviously being blamed for the performance against England. I didn't really know that I was one of them until the team was read out after training. It came as a great shock, but I'm not going to retire. When they dropped Charlie Faulkner the first thing he said was: "I shall return." I shall return too.'

Price was replaced by Eidman, of Cardiff. But though the going of Graham meant an end to international connections with the famed Pontypool front-row, there was solace for Price because two of the new young forwards were the latest from Prosser's production line at Pontypool. Jones replaced Williams at prop and Perkins took over from Moriarty, to win their first caps. The splendid Jackson was there to help Prosser celebrate. No doubt Pross punctuated his cheers with a few 'effs', as ever, but the *Mail* subbed them out. 'I intend to have,' Prosser told them, 'a bucketful of booze tonight. I'm not being unduly modest. I've been lucky to have got some really good players to work on. I'm delighted that Perky is getting his cap. He came to us ten years ago as a boy. He's hard and tough, a typically uncompromising Blaenavon man. Also I'm delighted for Staff Jones. All our international players have one thing in common – they came from nothing to get their caps, and that's great.'

Ireland, by contrast, kept faith with the veteran pack who had won them the Triple Crown the previous season and who had already this season heroically staved off defeat by Scotland. Now they awaited the championship favourites in Dublin. The French, two wins under their belt, arrived and, as is their custom, lay low in ominous wait for Saturday. They had dropped their half-backs after the Twickenham game and Delage and Berbizier were picked, to feed faster their dangerous backline. The tall catcher, Imbernon, returned at lock.

It was good to be back in Dublin after long winters of cricketing, though the soft weather of centuries was more chill than I can remember as the biting north-easterly yapped in from an ice-cold Irish Sea.

But the grass was a bright green and the sky a crisp, glistening blue. 'Ah,' enquired my purple-faced, jug-eared taximan, 'for the match, I suppose?' For the match, I said. 'Ah,' mused he, 'I don't know about the rugger, sor, but it's sure a lovely day for ploughin'. There'll be a lot out ploughing tomorrow.' But he agreed that no one would be out ploughin' come tomorrow afternoon. 'Every man, woman and child is keyed up. It does the old country good, does the rugger. Livens it up. They should play these games more often.'

The city has changed radically since I was last here. They have closed off Grafton Street to cars and everything else 'up there' is one-way. The Royal Hibernian Hotel has gone for good. Nobody could park nearby it, you see – 'you never used to be able to park up there at all, but now you can't park at all, at all,' my man said. I went to make sure one of my favourite shopsigns was still there 'Haircutting While-U-Wait'. The office-workers were taking brisk and animated constitutionals around Stephen's Green. The sacred smudge of ash from Wednesday was still on some foreheads, on the brow of solicitors and senators, and shining-faced secretaries with smiling Irish eyes and terrible Irish hang-ups. On their knees that morning, I fancy, more than a few candles were lit and prayers wafted up to Blessed Oliver Plunkett, the martyred seventeenth-century Bishop of Armagh, and patron saint of the Blessed Seamus Oliver Campbell, to whom many with their eyes on Lansdowne Road will be making their own individual prayers. Last winter Campbell's forty-six points ensured the Triple Crown for Ireland for the first time in twenty-five years. This season they are the only side who can win it again – indeed, a Grand Slam is within their grasp.

Last year in Paris the French stopped the Irish with – in the words of an editorial in a Dublin newspaper – 'head-bucking, gouging, boring, punching and similar skullduggery with the intent fully to send home the Irish forwards back across the sea in plastic bags.' So Saturday's match will be an occasion of terrible fury. But it's invariably tit-for-tat. As long ago as 1892 a J.J. McCarthy contributed thus an Irish chapter to the then

definitive volume *The Rugby Game*:

'Football in Ireland may be said to consist of three parts – Rugbeian, Associationist and Gaelic. The rule of play in these organisations had been defined as follows: in rugby, you kick the ball; in Association, you kick the man if you cannot kick the ball; and in Gaelic, you kick the ball if you cannot kick the man.' The rugger headquarters at Clonturk Park, McCarthy went on, was, 'conveniently situated between Glasnevin graveyard and the Mater Miserecordiae Hospital. A man has been known to pass from the football direct to the hospital, and from the hospital to the

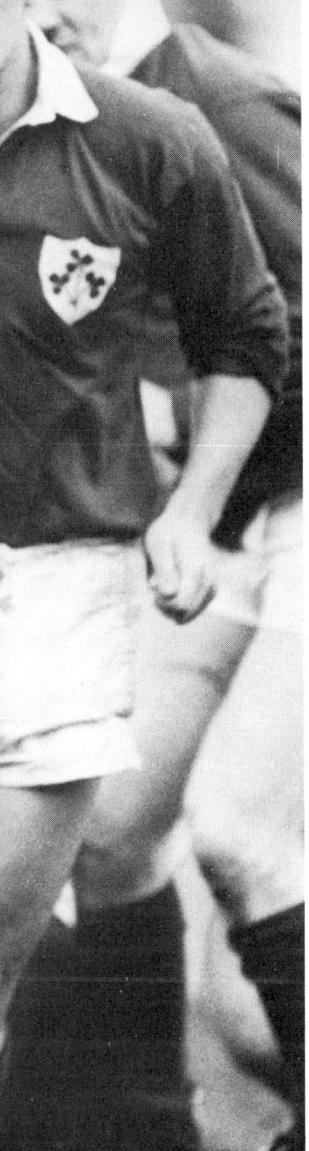

All year, Ireland's regular Army officer with the squaddie's face and determination was seldom away from the battlefront. 'Leadership,' says Fitzgerald, 'is reacting to the unexpected . . . having alternatives up your sleeve.' Ireland had a few – but would the Lions?

cemetery; another match being then got up to raise funds for the benefit of the next-of-kin, thus running the risk of killing a few more for the benefit of the deceased.'

In spirit at least, I reckon, things won't have changed much by tomorrow. The very thought of those first two or three scrums makes me wince. For the Irish are no angels, and their battle-scarred pack has been getting in first with the retaliation for a long time now. And when admonished – oh! the innocence of those open, guileless faces.

The stokers in the engine room this week have been working at more than just looking fierce, I can tell you. A stream of curses has been pouring forth as the eight-man juggernaut has clanked and clamped and charged itself up on the practice ground at Old Belvedere.

'Dad's Army' is led, of course, by that live regular Army captain, Ciaran Fitzgerald, squat and ferocious-looking with tree-trunk thighs, no neck and much charm. Fitzgerald was brought up on hurling and the aforesaid Gaelic stuff. He was born in Mayo in 1952 on 4 June, coincidentally the very day the Lions are due to play their first Test match against the All Blacks. He was brought up in County Galway where his father owned a garage. At twelve he came to Dublin to win a schools' boxing title, so early on he learned to take a thump in the face. At fifteen he was sent to Ballinasloe, to St Joseph's College. He had never even seen a rugger match but at once took to it – so heartily that when he left to go to the military college at The Curragh his games master, Fr John Kirby, forecast he would one day captain Ireland. He was well on the way to fulfilling the prophecy after he led the provincial minnows of Connacht to a stirring win over Munster in 1979. That was like me knocking out Henry Cooper.

Now this operations officer in the Second Infantry Battalion says captaincy on the rugby field is not unlike his daily preparations for leadership on the battlefield. 'All the preparation has been done before-hand. Leadership is reacting to the unexpected, choosing your options. You must always have alternatives up your sleeve: you must know when to turn on the tap, when to close it; when to accelerate, when to consolidate.' Before Fitzgerald came the other six in his platoon of eight must have thought they had won all the campaign medals they could. Their man inspired them to more.

From the deep green southern state where they also rear them to the tempests of Gaelic games come Moss Keane and Willie Duggan, thirty-five and thirty-three respectively. Slattery, the Blackrock boy who has laid waste more mid-field men than just about anyone in the game, is thirty-four. The two cornerstones, Phil Orr, the four-square Dubliner, and Gerry McLoughlin, flame-haired Limerick landlord of The Triple Crown bar, are both in their early thirties. The Stonyhurst public-schoolboy medic from Manchester, John O'Driscoll – a gentle fellow in civvies whom they call on the field 'O'Desperate' – has also seen the last of his twenties. One of the 'old' men's tasks tomorrow will be to defend the one youngster in their pack: if they do so he might well settle the thing, might Donal 'Loine-out' Lenihan, the twenty-three-year-old beanpole lock from Cork. They will hope to furnish Campbell with the where-withal. Campbell is much more than a kicker, of course. He has a beautiful pair of hands and feet with a delicate, deceptive pit-a-pat stride. The scrum-half Robbie McGrath is by no means the quickest nor the most

---

'You guys only ever print pictures of me as a kicker,' complains Campbell. 'But actually I think I do passing best.' Here O'Driscoll admires both the passing and running as first Pearce, then Winterbottom, crouch for the kill.

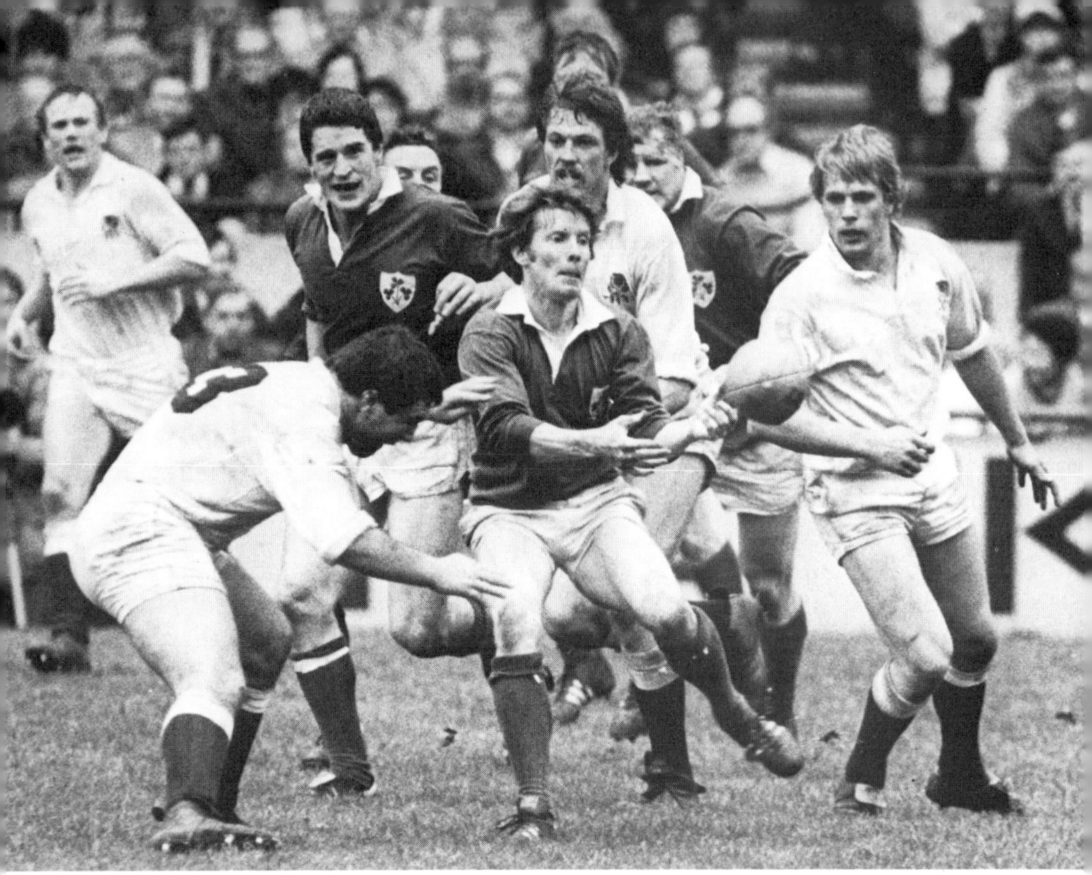

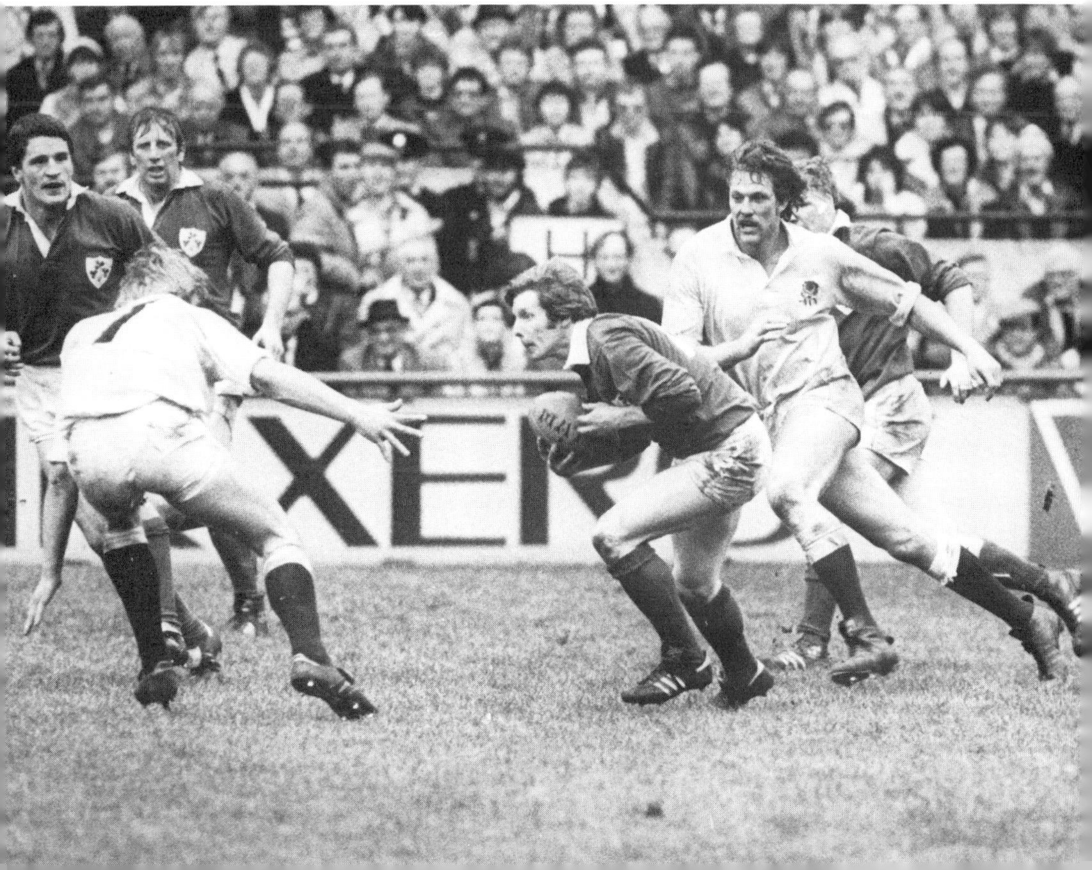

accurate passer with whom to be paired, yet he explained this week how last year they agreed on signals for an attempted drop goal. In the event, McGrath's pass squirted out at Campbell's bootlace – 'he was completely off balance and unready, yet he picked the thing off his toe, changed direction and intent in one stride, and took off on a mazy, bewildering run that presented a try to Moss Finn.'

Campbell is as shy as he is unaffected and friendly. He could pass, at a glance, for twenty: in fact he is thirty next year. To anyone else's knowledge he has no regular girlfriend. He works as salesman for the family's clothing firm. He still lives with Dad and Mam in the attractive Dublin suburb of Malahide. 'I'm spoiled, pampered, no doubt about it. I'm probably still tied to my mother's apron strings. If I come in late at night she'll always be up for me, just as if I was nine, not almost twenty-nine. No, she's never watched me play, since I was around fourteen. She won't even watch a recording of a match on television in case I'm murdered before her eyes!'

At Belvedere College old boys' ground on the Anglesea Road one can often find him alone at practice. Solitary. All weathers. Till the lights wink warm in the city yonder. Kick, kick, kick. Fetch and carry, fetch and carry. Kick, kick, kick. Short ones, long ones, wide ones, narrow ones. Fetch and carry, fetch and carry. Kick, kick, kick. Punting ones, torpedo ones, considered ones and hasty ones. He ends up with one from the halfway line, soccer's centre circle. He claws the mud from studs. With care he lines up his right instep against the ball, his left foot forward and alongside. He looks down at the ball, then up to gauge the distance. The goalposts are far away in the murk. Then, neither hurried nor too cautious, one-two-three-four-five steps back; a little one-and-a-half chassé sideways and left. A glance at the ball, the posts, then back to the ball. Up on his tiptoes just once, then a rhythmic, slightly curving run, eyes down, and . . . woompf! The 'H' is perfectly bisected.

Campbell's kicking is so prodigious that people in high places are talking about changing the rules and the points system. It's not a fair game when Ollie's around. Although he had been a schoolboy fly-half since he was nine he never kicked at goal – 'not even a 25 drop-out' – till he was seventeen. 'After that I got the taste – so started practising.' He does bridle shyly at being thought of only as a kicker – 'I actually think I do passing best,' he says. 'Though you lot would never write that, would you?'

Ned van Esbeck, doyen of the *Irish Times*, once explained how the boy had never sought to bargain with his talent: 'Ollie's a humble man. If he were locked up in a room or stuck in a lift with four other men for twenty-four hours they'd all come out of that room none the wiser as to who he was. They wouldn't even know he *liked* rugby football. His modesty is such that he wouldn't have even mentioned it.'

Last year, not long after Ireland had won the Triple Crown, there was celebrated in St Patrick's Cathedral, Dublin, an annual ecumenical service for sports folk. One of the lessons was read by Ollie Campbell. He chose a passage from the first epistle of St Paul to the Corinthians. Softly, reverently, he read: 'You know, do ye not, that at the sports all the runners run the race, though only one wins the prize. Like them, run to win. But every athlete goes into strict training. They do it to win a fading wreath; we, a wreath that never fades. For my part, I run with a clear goal before me; I am like a boxer who does not merely beat the air; I discipline my own body, and make it know its master, lest that by any means, having preached to others, I myself should be a failure.'

At Belvedere, he was taught by the Jesuit priest, Fr Jim Moran, who now works in Chicago. They are still in regular touch on the telephone. 'Don't let others define your pinnacles for you: set them yourself,' says Fr Moran. He would, however, always tell Ollie throughout his schooldays, 'Just because you are a good sportsman, don't think that makes you a better *person*,' and Campbell reflects on that to this day. 'Sure, I'm enjoying the rugby, though I admit the practising did once make me very blinkered. And it's nice to do well at it sometimes. But I know it's all a very temporary, transitory thing: soon, I know, I'll just fade into the distance and be an ordinary Joe Soap again.'

On the eve of the very confrontation itself I found myself sinking the black in the snug atmosphere of Sean Lynch's bar opposite Dublin's Carmelite Convent. Sean was a Lion of a prop who helped to bring the spoils home from New Zealand for Carwyn in 1971. But it was not to Sean that I was listening: in a wet-elbowed huddle, hammering out the ifs and buts and coulds and shoulds of the morrow, I was with none other than the Irish national coach himself, the old grey fox with the button snout, Tommy Kiernan.

Perhaps it was my Benedictine boyhood. Or an Irish father. But from the winter's day in 1960 that my uncle, who was from Cork, took me to Twickenham and introduced me to the boys from home I have ever worn the green weed on my sleeve on international days. We stayed at the Knights of St Columba Club in Kensington on the eve of the game and I remember that after midnight everyone stopped bibbing the black and started ordering Green Chartreuse. Next day everyone managed to be up for Mass. They were particularly looking to luck on account of it being a young Cork lad's first international. The Chartreuse and the heartfelt *Credo* worked wonders, for Tom Kiernan, from the Presentation College, had a wonderful game.

He had the kick of a Kinsale mule, the whooshing, deadly tackle of a midsummer Sligo scythe, and still a gentle open face as serene and warm as a turf fire in a cosy cottage. He went on to become the most capped full-back in international history. I worshipped him. Indeed, from that first day I was entranced by the way the Irish played the game. And they do it to this day: a hotchpotch of jigs and jinks and darts and delicate invention and wild make-do-and-mend and all the time maintaining the most furious gusto imaginable.

The Irish scrum-half for that first team I saw at Twickenham was a smart little sprite called Andy Mulligan, who combined a mischievous break with a deal of courage and a grand pass to his out-half. He later became a friend of mine (though I haven't seen him for ages: come back Mulligan, the fiver's forgotten) and once explained the philosophy behind the fizz of those Shamrock sides. Andy's first international was long before the days of squad systems, let alone men-of-the-match. He was understandably nervous before they left the dressing room. Two minutes to go and the captain finished doing up his laces and addressed them:

> 'Right, lads, let's decide how we're going to play this game. What do you think, Jack (Kyle)?'
> 'I think that a few wee punts at the line would be dandy, and maybe Mulligan here can try a few wee darts on his own.'
> 'What do you think, Tony (O'Reilly)?'
> 'Jasus, the programme here says I'm playing against a midget. Just let me have a run with the ball.'
> 'What about youse, Cecil (Pedlow)?'
> 'I think a subtle little mix of runnin' and kickin' and breakin' would be dandy.'
> The captain summed up: 'So it's decided, lads – Jack's puntin', Andy's dartin', Tony's runnin' and Cecil's doing all three.'

The whole philosophy was precisely presented back in the 1950s by the North of Ireland centre-threequarter, Noel Henderson, who was doubtless lacing up his boots during that very exchange that afternoon. Said Noel: 'The state of English and Welsh rugger is sometimes serious but never hopeless; the state of Irish rugby is usually hopeless but never serious.'

The enchanting amateur feel of Irish rugby was further summed up for me when Tony Ward showed me a long-ago letter written by the late Mai Purcell to an Irish fly-half of the fifties, Mick English, on the occasion of Mick's first international match. They worked together on the *Limerick Leader*. The memo went: 'Mickie – I should like to impress on you that I'm spending me whole week's wages, *viz* £3 .00, on the trip to Dublin just to see you play, and I beseech you not to make an eejit of yourself on this occasion. I furthermore request that on this auspicious afternoon, mindful of your duties and responsibilities, not only to your club and the people of Limerick, but to our country as a whole, that you keep y'bloody eye on the ball. Good luck, sir, and God Bless – Mai.'

The uncommitted will feel much the same as Mai these next two March Saturdays. Bejasus, what a hooley there'd be if they made it! It's high time they did. The Triple Crown is one glorious thing, the Grand Slam quite another – and how a Grand Slam for them would do the others good. They've won one this century – at Ravenhill, Belfast on 13 March 1948. Their winning try against Wales that day – a fly hack, an exuberant charge and a thudding bellyflop to a din that bounced all round the Mountains of

Mourne – was scored by a cumbersome prop-forward called Jack Daly. At the final whistle the green shirt was torn from his back and, as he was shouldered off in triumph, the socks peeled from his feet. And still, they will tell you, little square relics of fading green cloth are in existence, to be sure, framed in passepartout on mantelpiece shelves all over the little land, right next to the nightlight in front of the Sacred Heart and alongside the fluorescent statues of Our Lady brought back with the duty free from Lourdes or Lisieux. Y'man Daly, mind you, didn't need the shirt again – his name made, he at once caught a boat to Liverpool and cashed in with the rugby league.

Unless it's because their chroniclers appreciate adjectival colour more, Irish sides over the years seem to be packed with far more pungent personalities. As a character and raconteur, they say even Tony O'Reilly, auburn-haired fifties high flyer and another Belvedere old boy – 'We at Belvedere are tops at everything, including humility' – would be awarded the bronze medal behind two from the 1920s, the hunchy full-back Ernie Crawford and the roustabout, exuberant flanker, Jammie Clinch.

Crawford, whose rasping Belfast accent never left him in spite of a long Dublin domicile, invented the word 'alickadoo', that marvellous collective rugby noun covering all the game's hangers-on, administrators, selectors or bucket men for the Extra B . . . all those involved with the game who never play it.

The term originated on a train trip to London when Ernie failed to entice some other player to join the ritual game of poker. His colleague preferred to read a book which was about some oriental potentate. Ernie growled his displeasure: 'You and your bloody Ali Khadu!' After that, anyone who strayed from Ernie's conception of the proper order of affairs became an 'Alikadoo'.

In 1924 Jammie Clinch toured South Africa with the Lions. His mentor was a *pukka* Englishman from Blackheath, A. F. 'Blakey' Blakiston. One time Jammie laid low a particularly troublesome Springbok forward – but a tough Afrikaaner who was quick to recover and get back on his feet. 'That's no good, old boy,' said Blakey to Jammie – 'jab your fingers in his eye when he's goin' down and he won't get up so readily.' The following season, England v Ireland at Twickenham, the two pirates were in opposition. Late in the match a group of white-jerseyed English players stood around the fallen Blakey when Jammie pushed his way in, presumably to discover the extent of his friendly rival's injuries. Jammie gazed down at the recumbent warrior and inquired innocently: 'Did I do it right that time, Blakey?'

In a nation of funny men, of bawdy bards and genius journalists, even one of the greatest of them all, Myles na Gopaleen, was partial to his rugger. Here he is meeting Jammie Clinch in a bar in 1959, and, naturally, discussing tactics:

'Ever hear of "the Box"? (I didn't say the 'Boks.) That crowd decided that, after a scrum, there was no future in passing the ball to a string of centres and wings, but to get it to the blind side of the scrum and get it to "the box", an area practically devoid of defence. The result of this conspiracy was a plethorium of scoretown. Ah, but shure I might as well be talking to the wall. Mick, two more pints!'

'Clinch. They call me "Jammie" Clinch.'

'Ah. So? Then you must know my pupils Farrell, Sugden, Davy, Pike, Stephenson? Promising lads, one and all. I, too, have played of course.'

'Rugby? For Ireland? Well . . . by gob!'

'Ah yes. I turned out in the first game against France in 1909. Odd, isn't it, that the 1959 match will be the fiftieth encounter. France had some very clever men in those days, Jauréguy for instance, or Cassayet. Glad to see you are turning out yourself. I suppose you know what a rugby ball is?'

'A what? It's an oval affair.'

'No. Oval connotes a plane configuration; you could never pick anything oval up, or kick it. You might, perhaps, do something with an ovoid. In fact, a rugby ball is a prolate speroid.'

'I never knew that was what I scored with.'

It was an early morning to remember. Omens were good for the morrow and my only worry was whether I would be too bleary to savour the day. I was, as it happened, up early enough in Buswell's . . . but, alas, one pilgrimage is off the list, with the going of the Royal Hibernian, and so to sniff the congenial flavours there can now be no more morning promenade in the footsteps of another great Campbell – the late Paddy – who once so gloriously chronicled the days of the 1930s when the boys in green were due to kick off at 2.15. It would begin in the basement of the Hibernian outside the door of the Buttery – 'almost always as early as 10.25, to be in good time for the throwing-open of the portals at 10.30'. Once they were inside, service would be delayed by George and Jack behind the bar in discussion with the older members about 'What would be good for it?' 'It', of course, was the accumulated result of the two days and nights of conjecture about the possible result of the coming match: not a matter to be lightly dismissed.

This morning in 1983, I at least doffed my cap and white-frothed my top lip with 'just the one' as genuflection at Davy Byrne's to Campbell and his pilgrims from half a century ago. For them, by around eleven, a number would decide it was high time to see what was going on in Davy Byrne's just around the corner, followed – about 11.45 – by an investigation into Bailey's Hotel, almost opposite, a smooth flow that led them into Jammett's back bar as early as 12.30. Seeing that at that chilly hour it was much too soon for lunch the more socially-minded of them nipped around the corner of Nassau Street and back into the Buttery, where to many it seemed they had only been a minute or two before. And so they would repeat the route.

But as Campbell said, 'All this wasn't simply a vulgar drunken rout. It was much more the marvellous excitement at feeling the whole city *en fête*, that hundreds of thousands of people had abandoned care, work, wives and other encumbrances and were making devotedly, if circuitously, for the ultimate Mecca of Lansdowne Road.'

And after that, with a breakfast on the way at the Shelbourne with my friends, Lander of the *Mirror*, Todd of the *Sun* and Edwards of ITN, we proceeded down past Doheny & Nesbitt's and Gratton's, where we took another oncer and some warming stew with a bright-eyed friend of mine from years gone by who used to work for Aer Lingus, who is called Jeannie and without a word of a lie has got light brown hair . . .

At last, to Lansdowne Road. The crowds cram in. There were rumours that six thousand counterfeit tickets had been printed – and were being used. The An Garda Siochana band tinkled and blew, and did the occasional soft-shoe shuffle in unison – almost, you felt, in their sleep. Then the Fintan Lalor Pipe Band had a whistle. The gulls sailed and squealed over the misty distance that shrouded cranes, spires and, away to my left, a rusty, circled cluster of gasometers; an ancient anachronism, an industrial Stonehenge. The Garda ended with 'The Saints Go Marching In'. For a moment, silence; then a roar as the gladiators take to the amphitheatre. No anthems now in Dublin – too evocatively dangerous – no Soldier's Song. No *Queen* even for the two Ulstermen of the XV, Irwin and Ringland. Not a *Marseillaise* for Rives's. Just on with the mayhem and motley, as, in Roy McFadden's 'Garryowen' poem, 'In forced tumescent waves the faceless crowd/Washes the field with sublimating sound;/ Implores, deplores, ejaculates aloud./On, up and under, forwards. Charge the line.'

France made a hash of their start. Within a minute Campbell had missed a thirty-five-yard sighting pot at goal – but then within three minutes he had landed an even closer one after another over tense charge by Paparemborde. Nine minutes later he put over another – and the whole congregation, convulsed and delirious, knew that their kicker had overtaken Kiernan's points record for Ireland. In fifty-four matches Kiernan scored 158 points. In just eighteen matches Campbell had overtaken it. That is why men want to change the rules for Campbell. It is dotty, to be sure, if kickers are to dominate a handling game.

Blanco retrieved three of those points before Campbell made it 9–3 – and then the fly-half's up and under into 'the box' had France in palpitations on their twenty-five. The Irish won the ball, spun it left and, with MacNeill haring into the line, Finn had room to dart over. The conversion made France's second half task a daunting one, and at 15–3 there seemed good reason fcr 'Sweet Molly Malone' to waft up, serenely, into the mists. The gulls glided, or squawked, to the lilt.

But the French were to rally with stupendous vim. Or, rather, Blanco did. First he bazookered a penalty from the halfway line: 15–6. Then he swept into the line, going left. Esteve was boxed in, Blanco chipped through – low and delicate and as precise as Trevino into the wind. He galloped on to touch down and, converting the thing himself from halfway out, made it 15–12 – a very different affair. Dry throats turned from 'Molly Malone'. Fitzgerald was limping now, and indeed the whole Irish pack looked whacked – the more so when Esteve, looping into the centre, kicked ahead, found the bounce with him and scored another try: 15–16, and the French seemingly unstoppable. Just quarter of an hour remained. France came again: Blanco, Blanco all the way; Belascain fumbled; MacNeill, desperate, hacked at the bobbing ball . . . suddenly it was deep and dangerous inside French territory. Blanco and all France had to turn. MacNeill hacked on; the nippy Sella raced back, fell on the ball barely ten yards from his line; MacNeill was on him, the Irish pack fast behind. They won it, the movement went left and Finn was over in the corner – to tumult. Campbell missed the conversion, but sealed an historic victory with a penalty just before the end. Begob and glory be! 22–16.

Then we heard that Wales had beaten Scotland at Murrayfield by 19–15 – apparently a deserved result after a workmanlike performance: Holmes, as ever, a host unto himself. But their afternoon was illuminated by a try, sponsored on the left by Clive Rees and finished on the right by his namesake, Elgan. Between the two of them the ball had been handled in turn by Dacey, Butler, Ackerman, Richards and Wyatt.

And so when Ireland play Wales in Cardiff in a fortnight the thing was set for another truly tempestuous occasion. Yet in this last quarter of an hour the venerable Irish pack played themselves to such a standstill that I seriously suggest they might not have recovered by the time they travel to the rejuvenated Welsh.

In the set scrums and line-outs France had licked the Irish hollow. By midway through the second half victory for the Irish could only be won by guts and fervour and madcap mayhem. Through the final ferocious passages one could hear the fervent exhortation: 'C'mon boys, c'mon.

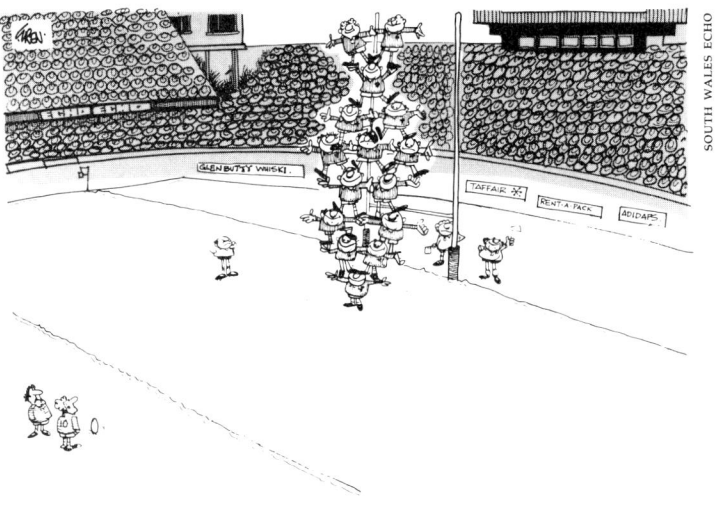

"Begorrah Ollie – I tink dey've rumbled our tactic."

Not long left, boys. Y'doing grand. For Ireland, boys!' Looking more like a nightclub bouncer or boxer who'd lost his licence, Ciaran Fitzgerald would shake his fist at his man, or walk down the line-out before throwing-in with a slap of encouragement on each of seven bottoms. 'C'mon, let's give it one more go, boys!'

Much later, showered and blazered, his Wolfhounds tie proving that there is a neck in there somewhere, he was swigging his bottle of Smethwicks and rejoicing in the afternoon's play. 'By Jove, they have a terribly strong set scrum. 'Twas a magnificent physical contest all through, a most rewarding experience to be part of.' Wasn't it a touch dirty in that front-row? 'Not at all; no messing about at all.' He could have fooled me. What about his own injury? ' 'Twas nothing. Me knee just twisted out of its socket for a moment or two.' He called for another Smethwicks – just as he had done deep into the night before at Sean Lynch's bar. Fitzgerald indeed is in the Lynch tradition.

His rival captain, Rives, sat dejected, disappointed but chivalrous. 'A good victory. They deserve. I think they play in the Irish tradition. It was difficult; Ireland's tradition is to play as near as it is possible to the ball. If the ball is over the line they are first . . .' And he gave a little shrug, and a little giggle. *Eh, voila!*

In the *Irish Press* that very morning Cormac MacConnell had implored Rives and his Frenchmen to lose on purpose: 'We the Irish, never lower in spirit or morale, are totally dependent for our social and economic future upon Ciaran Fitzgerald's team to raise and heal our broken hearts and minds.' It was only half in jest. Consider the facts, he wrote. They were bankrupt. They were politically and geographically divided. They were disgraced internationally by a whole range of issues ranging from tapping and bugging to the kidnapping of harmless stallions. Fianna Fail lay in splinters, the Northern Assembly in ruins, while the Coalition Government was rapidly falling asunder on a matter of life and death. They were overtaxed, over-wrought, overstressed, and only in the matter of murdering each other, robbing banks and plotting against their leaders had they recently shown true Gaelic style.

'Every time Fitzgerald wins a strike against the head a score of different strikes in the industrial world are forgotten and 10,000 heads lift with pride, North and South. And every time the props heave powerfully the props of our entire national structures are made less vulnerable. And every time Ollie Campbell lands a penalty all of us tend to forget, however briefly, many of the daily penalties of living in this troubled land, lately so close to every wooden spoon on offer. I would, therefore, appeal to our French visitors, who do everything with great flair and style, to somehow contrive today to lose this game narrowly, gallantly and with style. It is quite within their compass and it would be marvellous altogether if they could manage to build up a first half lead, then fail to subdue the Irish fight-back over the last ten minutes.'

And so – more or less – it came to pass.

CHAPTER NINE

Diminuendo

While we were waiting for the fortnight to go before Ireland attempted to get past halfway in their Grand Slam bid there was an awful lot of sound and fury down in the dungeons as England and Scotland prepared to play for the wooden spoon. Predictably England dropped their captain, Smith, and chose the younger, faster Melville. They also dropped Cusworth for John Horton, the experienced Bath fly-half who had played in Beaumont's 1980 side. This seemed needless and desperately unfair on Cusworth, an inventive and stealthy player who was noticeably improving as he had settled in through the four months he had played. Then Melville injured his ankle at training and Smith was recalled. 'I told you they'd have to nail down my coffin,' he announced chirpily as he posed for press pictures clinking glasses with his successor as captain, John Scott. Wheeler had been overlooked as captain again: someone obviously knew something that nobody else did. Wheeler congratulated Scott, who now had a chance to captain the Lions; but Fitzgerald had become the runaway favourite.

Meanwhile Scotland, too, changed their captain, replacing Laidlaw with the doughty prop, Aitken. Laidlaw kept his place at scrum-half and was joined in relaxed partnership with the accomplished John Rutherford, who had at last recovered from the injury which had him missing the first two internationals. As it turned out, Scotland played splendidly, won the Calcutta Cup with ease, and at times, by all accounts, came near to humiliating England. Certainly 22–12 suggests a comprehensive victory. Rutherford played calmly, Laidlaw with typical zest, and Aitken's noticeably inspiring leadership made Scott's look flabby and dull. Two male streakers, who were later charged, and two female streakers, who were not – they were never intercepted by the police – showed more speed and swerve than any of the English backs.

Ireland, meanwhile, blew up in Cardiff. One had half suspected that the dynamic form the venerable pack had summoned in Dublin could not be sustained with scarcely a fortnight's rest. Not that the Irish didn't whirr the shillelagh with keenness: only this time it kept whizzing back to catch

The Debutant's Ball . . . In his first match, Scotland's Smith flops down to score direct from a line-out – the final humiliation to cap England's tattered season.

them, embarrassed and off-balance. Campbell, for once, played an edgy, nervous game; so did his captain, Fitzgerald, whose line-out throwing was askew, so much so that Norster cleaned up, to poor young Lenihan's bewilderment. By all accounts, Fitzgerald's throwing into the line had been exemplary in the desperate close match at Murrayfield, but here his aim to the jumpers was frequently inaccurate. For Wales, Price returned for the injured Eidman – triumphantly. The old boy was inspired. Also, the Welsh had Holmes. The tide of the whole piece ebbed and flowed around this superlative player. He displayed a devious, often inspired nous at the base of the scrum; as well, of course, as an ox-like strength.

A half-time lead to Wales of 12–6 – answering penalty goals decorated by a Wyatt try, forged, polished and presented by Holmes – was not irretrievable, but Campbell of all people marginally knocked-on from the kick-off and a scrum on the line was all that Holmes required to bullock over and put Ireland out of reach at 16–6. Comparisons now with Gareth are not sacrilege when revelling in Holmes's talent. Wyatt played beautifully to make a third try for Elgan Rees and Wales won by a comprehensive 23–9. In eighty minutes, alas, before our very eyes, the ageing Irish

Diminuendo

"GOT SOMETHING SUITABLE FOR A WELSH SELECTOR? ANYTHING IN BRAILLE WILL DO?"

aged. I thought of Tom Reid, the lovable Garryowen forward of the fifties. That, said the referee, was a late tackle. 'Sorry, sor,' panted Tom. 'I got there as fast as I could.' The war is over; Dad's Army will never summon up more now than warm, nostalgic memories – and, for sure, effort enough for one last farewell victory over the demoralised English in a fortnight's time at Lansdowne Road.

That they duly did – 25–15. And, as they say, England were lucky to get fifteen! Smith had been dropped again – and wasn't even a reserve – and Youngs, the Leicester scrum-half, replaced the still injured, unlucky Melville. Hare again played well: there was little else that moved in white. Campbell scored six goals in nine attempts for Ireland and also an opportunist's try – to bring his season's points tally to fifty-two and so to beat his own record of forty-six in a Championship campaign. England were in shreds. Not often have beginning-of-the-season favourites been so collectively laid low. Ireland could only draw the Championship, however – and only then if France beat Wales in Paris. If Wales won that match they would, astonishingly, win the title outright. After their traumas of last season, and much of this, even their hardiest supporters could scarcely credit such a result.

For Paris Price retained his place at prop – the city in which he had not only made the first of his forty-one appearances but had scored a glorious solo sprinter's try eight years before. Whether Price's surprising omission against Scotland was an aberration on the part of the selectors or a ploy to shake him out of some supposed complacency one could only guess –

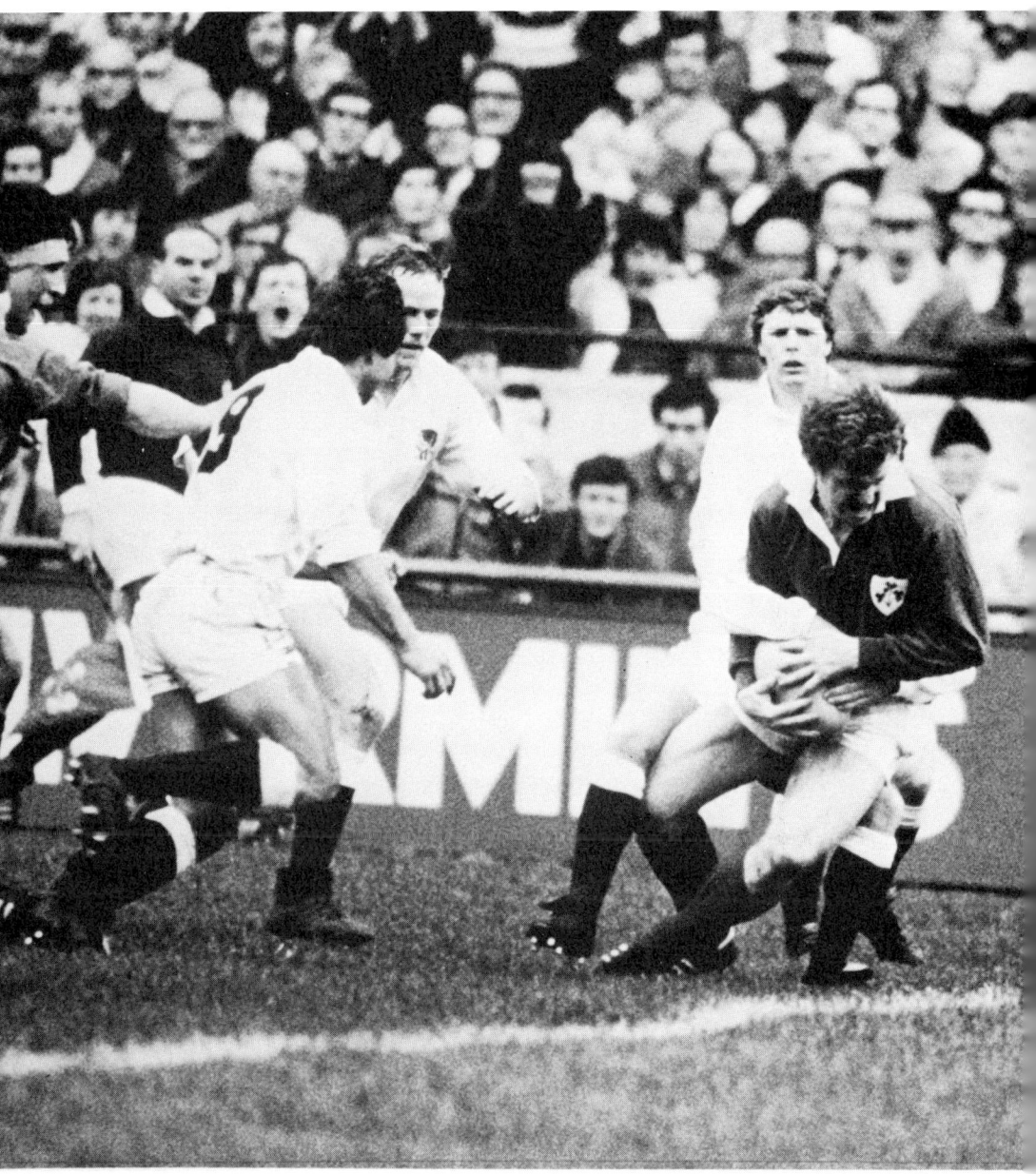

For probably the last of many occasions Fergus Slattery's quicksilver anticipation takes England by surprise and he opens the scoring in Dublin. The play of the legendary flanker at the end of his 14th international season once more gave the lie to the Irish pack's collective title 'Dad's Army'.

though Price was recalled, remember, only when Eidman pulled out. But it worked and, with his two young 'Poola' tyros, Jones and Perkins, alongside and behind him, they had quite discomfited Ireland. Before that game the chairman of the selectors, Clive Rowlands, had picked on Price as the team prepared to take the field. Jabbing his fingers fiercely into Price's badged three feathers, Rowlands sneered – 'You, Price. A record forty caps indeed! You haven't deserved one of them, you know. Not one!' Price was used to Prosser, but this was something altogether more needling. Rowlands went on as every other player quaked. 'Forty caps? Don't make me laugh. Not one deserved! And you'll only deserve the one you get today if you go out there on to that field and prove it to me! Go out there, Price, and prove it to Wales!' And of course, so bidden, Price did.

Since he was Welsh captain nearly twenty years ago, Rowlands has become increasingly famed for his dressing-room pep talks – or rather, raging fire-and-brimstone rhetoric. Not a player dares flex a muscle; new caps stop breathing and suddenly realise why Rowlands is called 'Topcat'. For when Rowlands's oratory is in the trim then so, often, is Wales's belief in themselves.

Cowering in the corner during such tirades is the one other 'civilian' allowed in the holy of holies. At Murrayfield last month Gerry Lewis made his 100th appearance. One of his multitude of jobs will be to rush out at an injury with his bucket of water – 'good Welsh tap water, boy' – and magic sponge at the slightest suggestion of a wilting or wounded Welshman. 'No, don't be silly, plain cold water dóes do good. It compresses the wound, freezes it.'

'Physiotherapist' covers a litany of virtues, not least of which is chaplain and father confessor. He has been much loved by successive Welsh teams since his first match twenty-two years ago, when he was just thirty. For fifteen years before him his father, Ray, held the same, honorary post.

If Rowlands's pumping hywl represents the crescendo of the afternoon's overture in the inner sanctum, Gerry Lewis has long set up the full solemnity of the occasion. He greets each player with a handshake and, eyes lowered, hands them their gleaming new scarlet shirt. Other international teams just have them hanging on a peg. Gerry has pressed and folded his with the Prince of Wales motif as the centrepiece. He hands them over like a priest at the offertory in pontifical high mass. 'I gave Gareth more than fifty shirts. Unfailingly, he would solemnly kiss first the feathers on the badge, then kiss me on both cheeks. Barry would receive his, then silently, movingly, hug me. Charlie Faulkner, mind, would throw his in the air and say, "Effing 'eck, I've got another one."'

On Thursday night, after practising in Cardiff, the team went to the film *Gandhi*. They flew to Paris this – Friday – morning and tonight there will be another compulsory show. Lewis will be tempted to creep away once the lights go down and nip off to the opera. He hopes it might be Gounod's *Faust*, his favourite, which he had been taken to at the age of five. In the early sixties, on his first visit with the Welsh team to Paris, he saw Callas in *Carmen*. 'What an actress! What a voice!' He still sings in his bath or in the team bus – a bit of a come-down for a youthful nightingale.

When he was ten, he was Benjamin Britten's principal boy soprano and once he packed them in at London's Wigmore Hall, when his pianist was Dame Myra Hess. After school at Pontywaun he went down the pit at Oakdale and Risca as a packer – shoring up the roof, payment by the yard and sometimes working in little over two and a half feet headroom. When he emerged into daylight he played on the wing for Cross Keys. 'Yes, I'd love to have been a Ken Jones or Dewi Bebb or Gerald but, to be honest, I'd much rather have been Pavarotti singing at La Scala.' His father had fired in him an interest in physiotherapy, but National Service sponsored it with a full training course. With his wife, Val, he now runs at Newport probably the biggest physio clinic in Wales.

Grandfather was a minister in the chapel. Gerry inherits some shining sort of saintliness. He says the only time in his life he 'nearly' lost his temper was with Colin Meads, the legendary All Black: 'He was a giant on the field and a perfect gent off it, but this time he kneed Clive Rowlands in the back to displace his fourth lumbar disc. I said there was no need for that, and Meads replied, "It's a man's game. If he can't take it then he shouldn't play it."' Rowlands was carried off, not to play again for the rest of the season.

In his famous little black bag Gerry holds two sizes of Elastoplast, bandages, Vaseline, Deep Heat and smelling salts. He doesn't believe in freeze sprays. Deep down among the linament is a Bible. 'A New Testament – never without it. Our Welsh boys are the greatest rugby men of all, but for some reason they are much quicker than anyone else to get homesick and are a little afraid to say, "I want to go to church or to chapel and sing some hymns like I did when I was young." Sometimes they just want to chat about all the values they knew at home, so then my Bible comes in handy.'

The grandson of the Manse is ecumenical now.

Once, when he was in charge of the Welsh team at a 'B' international, played in Lourdes, the French religious shrine, he announced the night before that he was planning to attend Mass in the Basilica the following morning. Who wanted to accompany him? 'Get stuffed, Gerry!' cried the team in unison. Okay, said Gerry, but if any of you change your mind I'll be leaving the foyer sharp at twenty minutes to nine. And so he did – followed by nineteen of the squad of twenty-one!

Now, in Paris, new prayers had been said and shirts presented. Topcat has had his say, and Lewis is ready to lead out his latest class of '83. From the dressing-room door to the mouth of the tunnel the tradition is to follow him. Before he opens the dungeon door he has one final check on his own outfit. Always a suit or a blazer. He is not a tracksuit manager, another trait that stems from his father. 'He was ill in hospital when I took over from him. "Remember this," he said, "and remember it well – you

When injuries allowed, Holmes on the break was one of the most thrilling, surging sights of the era. Playing alongside Wales's original and virile scrum-half, says his captain, Butler, was 'like being carried along in a back row of five men'.

Esteve, as delicate as he is fast, scored in every Championship match for France. Here he escapes yet again to down the ball in his favourite corner of Paris, and Ackerman (13) and all France know Wales are done for.

are a professional man in your own right so act like one always, behave like one always, and dress like one always.''' At the meeting of the tunnel and the touchline he will step aside and let his Scarlets charge. He has a slap on the backside for each of them; and says fifteen times: 'It's for Wales!' So Gerry does in fact have the last word. To be honest, he admits, he is the least frightened man present when Topcat starts his pre-match screeching. He knows Clive will never pick on him – after all, in 1963, he presented Rowlands with his first-ever Welsh jersey.

Alas, none of the Topcat's oratory, none of Gerry's ritual with the shirts works this time. It is a day for getting out the Bible. It is a terribly disappointing match, a seedy, ill-mannered affair from the very first, hornlocking scrum. It was, perhaps, unfair to ask a visiting referee, Tom Dooley, of New Zealand, to handle such a tense decider. He had also been in charge of the Calcutta Cup match a fortnight previously: in that he had awarded only sixteen penalties and ignored most of the line-out malpractices: here in Paris he gave thirty-five penalties (3–1 in France's favour), but still turned a blind eye to the line-out and much else besides. Meanwhile the bloody affair – literally, for Rives's white jersey was spattered red from the first minutes – swirled on down below us. Squire scored an opening, blindside, battering-ram of a try to raise Welsh hopes, but with relentless strength the French pack heaved their way into total command. Just on half time Wyatt broke his collar bone – a tragedy for his Lions' aspirations – though by then the Welsh were on the rack. They held on heroically enough as penalties were swapped, but the increasingly rampant French bided their time and, after a debatable 'carry-over' decision had given them a five-yard scrum halfway out, they fingertipped the ball to the deadly finisher, Esteve, and he dropped it down in his favourite corner. Blanco celebrated with two late, joyous penalty goals to seal it at 16–9.

All in all, it was a rotten, roguish match. At the end, as is the tradition, the two teams fell on each others' necks, looking – their cuts and cauliflowered ears notwithstanding – as guiltless as choir boys. I was reminded of when Max Baer fought Joe Louis. Between rounds Max's second encouraged him: 'Don't worry, kid, he hasn't hit you once.' Through bloodied lips, Max dolefully inquired: 'Well, this round keep an eye on that ref, because somebody in there sure is beating hell outta me!'

Long before the end of this game – and, with it, the Championship – the malevolent atmosphere had made the result immaterial. You did not care who won as long as peace and friendship would break out soon. The French obviously had the same feeling, although they looked at it in a slightly different light. As we woke blearily next day an eight-column newspaper headline, as well as the placards that dotted the boulevards, had it, in a trumpeting salute to their warriors: 'ILS LONT GAGNÉ COMME À VERDUN'.

This was where I came in – an interview with Jean-Pierre Rives. Probably my last with him. Throughout his (surely?) final afternoon, white shirt turned pink, he had looked like an abattoir operative on piecework. His head still leaked blood. He nodded sagely. 'It was,' said this master of understatement, 'a very bad game for to play in.'

But then the whole five-nations season, on which I had embarked with such refreshing anticipation in Toulouse five months ago, had been no great shakes. There had been one or two electric moments – England's try at Cardiff, Wales's at Murrayfield – but the only match of stirring quality that I saw was when France were repelled in Dublin; so it was fitting, I suppose, that those two combatants shared the title – though this curtain-call from France was an unnecessary appendage.

Only next week's showpiece in Edinburgh – Scotland against the Barbarians – can spray on a bit of freshness and save a generally lacklustre season. There we would look to have the blinkers off, a hatful of tries – and then, of course, we discover if lambs can become Lions . . .

CHAPTER TEN

The Old Stamping Ground

McBride and Telfer, manager and coach to the 1983 British Lions, both stared out stonily from behind a table in the smoke room of the East India Club in London's St James. Between them sat a middle-aged Staffordshire vet with a no-nonsense, haughty bearing and fiery eyes under Denis Healey eyebrows. 'Gentlemen, I will simply read out the team we have selected,' said Micky Steele-Bodger, chairman of the Home Union's Tours Committee, and eminence gruff of Twickenham's establishment. Bodger carefully read the names in positional order and with full initials.

Us hacks scribbled: 'Full-Backs: W. H. Hare (Leicester & England). H. P. MacNeill (Blackrock College, Oxford University & Ireland). Right-Wings: J. Carleton (Orrell & England). T. M. Ringland (Ballymena & Ireland). Left Wings: G. R. T. Baird (Kelso & Scotland). G. Evans (Maesteg & Wales). Centres: R. A. Ackerman (London Welsh & Wales). D. G. Irwin (Instonians & Ireland). M. J. Kiernan (Dolphin & Ireland). C. R. Woodward (Leicester & England). Stand-Offs: S. O. Campbell (Old Belvedere & Ireland). J. Y. Rutherford (Selkirk & Scotland).

'Props: S. T. Jones (Pontypool & Wales). I. Stephens (Bridgend & Wales). I. G. Milne (Heriot's FP & Scotland). G. Price (Pontypool & Wales). Hookers: C. T. Deans (Hawick & Scotland). C. F. Fitzgerald (St Mary's College & Ireland, captain). Locks: S. B. Boyle (Gloucester & England). M. J. Colclough (Angôuleme & England). D. G. Lenihan (Cork Constitution & Ireland). R. L. Norster (Cardiff & Wales). Flankers: J. H. Calder (Stewart's Melville FP & Scotland). P. J. Winterbottom (Headingley & England). J. B. O'Driscoll (Manchester & Ireland). J. Squire (Pontypool & Wales). No. 8s: J. R. Beattie (Glasgow Academicals & Scotland). I. A. M. Paxton (Selkirk & Scotland).

'Officials: Manager, W. J. McBride (Ireland). Assistant Manager & Coach, J. W. Telfer (Scotland), Doctor, D. A. D. MacLeod (Scotland). Physiotherapist, K. Murphy (England).'

There had been a noticeable, collective intake of breath at the first syllable of, alphabetically, the second hooker. 'Fitz . . .' was all we wanted to hear. Wheeler was not even in the team. The Irishman was captain. We had got our story – and the spongy tread of a dozen Hush Puppies was already beating a path across the polished parquet to the two public telephones on the first floor of the stately old club. McBride had solemnly been filling his pipe with the strong-man's mixture, Condor, all through the announcement. Now he spoke: 'When you look at the form of the four home countries over the past two seasons the leadership was pretty well a foregone conclusion.' He added defiantly, 'Ciaran Fitzgerald is a proven leader of men.'

Then, at one and the same time, Willie-John jutted his jaw and relit his pipe. Those of us waiting for the telephones considered who else had been unlucky not to make the trip – Robertson, the Scottish centre, was certainly on most people's lists, and some were still championing the two flankers, Leslie of Scotland and Jeavons of England. But there was nothing much else to get worked up about. Wheeler's omission – the player learned about it when he stepped off the ferry at Liverpool on his way back from England's weekend debacle in Dublin – was the news. Next day, even the *Guardian* had an editorial about it: 'The history of British sport is strewn with examples of players chosen for their ability as captains who have not proved their comparable worth as players. Usually the tour results have not been successful, including, it may be remembered, the occasion when the captaincy of the Lions by the Irish hooker Ronnie Dawson meant that Bryn Meredith, widely regarded as the best all-round forward in the world, was relegated to the Wednesday team. Australia and New Zealand manage these affairs differently. There is no doubt that Ciaran Fitzgerald is a good, committed hooker of a type that abounds in world rugby. But Peter Wheeler combines high specialist skills with the strength and combativeness in ruck and maul of a prop forward or a lock, and hookers like this are rare in the post-war history of the game: Meredith, certainly, Bert Godwin of Coventry and England possibly. To dispense with such a precious and proven asset in New Zealand looks wilfully perverse.'

This brought a nice letter back to the editor from a Mr A. E. Cameron, of London: 'Sir – Captains of the quality of Ciaran Fitzgerald do not abound in world rugby (though hookers may) and his qualities of leadership have brought a fairly average Ireland team two very successful seasons. Who is the best hooker available? Rugby writers on the French sporting newspaper *L'Equipe* had little doubt: in a team selected from the five championship nations they chose four Irishmen, three Welshmen, no Englishmen and only one Scot; Colin Deans of Hawick as hooker. Yours faithfully . . .'

The rest of the week, thank heaven, afforded the opportunity to get back to the fledgling roots of the game – at the annual schoolboys' gala in Roehampton, the Rosslyn Park seven-a-side tournament. My old school, Douai, now competes in the Festival competition – for schools who play hockey or soccer in the Easter term – but, alas, as has often happened in recent years, they were eliminated early on, certainly by the time I turned up. Interest remained for a Benedictine, because Ampleforth, the black-cowled giants from the north, were on course to repeat their astonishing double of 1977 by winning both the Festival series and the Open tournament for the serious big-timers. In the event they won the first and were beaten only by Millfield in the latter final – a tremendous effort.

In my day the tournament organisers insisted the event was called the 'Public Schools Sevens', which made us insufferable lot from minor establishments puff up pimply cheeks with misplaced pride. The first time I took my boots there in the middle fities I was reserve for Douai. In the first round we played Radley. Tense in the dressing room, our Benedictine coach, Fr Wulstan, told us to take it easy on them because we had a lot of games before the next day's final. We lost that opening match 37–0! At fourteen minutes a game that was nearly a try a minute. Next year we did much better, and the season after I left Douai won the thing. In fact, what with Douai, Downside, Ealing, Ampleforth, Belmont and Worth, the Benedictines have a good record in the event. Our sportsmasters might like to believe it was something to do with St Benedict's emphasis on obedience.

The tournament has changed a lot . . . at first glance, anyway. Girlfriends turn up now. Everyone is clothed in the ubiquitous denim. The boys are allowed to have their hair cut any old how and some even sport moustaches. Ever since Rosslyn Park, the organisers, rightly allowed them in, the grammar schools have more than proved their worth. I remember when Llanelli Grammar School withdrew in the sixties because they were winning so regularly. The first time I reported the event, in the middle of the sixties, I watched a square little bull from Millfield perform the most crazy charges; he was unstoppable. Afterwards, I asked him his name. 'Edward,' I thought he said. 'Edward who?' 'No, sir, Edwards with an "s". My first name's Gareth.' Note that one: who else in sport has Gareth called 'sir'?

It was an experience I missed, actually playing in *the* Sevens as a schoolboy. I was not fast enough, I suppose, and certainly an airy-fairy tackler. Still, I notice, 'genuine' scrum-halves do not always get a game in sevens. The fashion often is to put a runner or even a hard-nut forward there. Years ago, apparently, at the Middlesex sevens, the Harlequins played that uncompromising England scrummager, Vic Marriott, at scrum-half. Outside him was the gregarious Joe McPartlin, of Oxford and Scotland. Afterwards Joe explained the partnership: 'I didn't too much mind getting the ball along the ground all the time, or even having to fall on it, but the thing that worried me was when I did go down it was always Marriott who was the first to kick me in the back.' Happy days.

And more, too, are expected this weekend – in Edinburgh. There can be no denying that the standards of British international rugby are low, but it is fervently hoped the Barbarians will celebrate in festive style against Scotland in the gala that officially opens Murrayfield's new grandstand. The old city never changes – the stadium has. Scotland were the first country to buy their own ground, at Inverleith in 1879. They acquired Murrayfield's vast acres sixty years ago and opened with a 14–11 victory against England in 1925.

I went to see the stand on the way from the airport: it is an unweathered Meccano job, block concrete and sweeping struts; smart, swank and un-Scottish. So a season that started with official piety about Adidas revelations ends with a match organised solely to pay for a new stand. In Paris last week every player had the distinctive markings on his boots. The match ball had the name, Adidas, branded all over it. Only England get at the black Cherry Blossom before a game. Only Twickenham have resisted a sell-out festival match to pay for their new stand.

Scotland have had another disappointing international winter, yet they probably had the best British side of the quartet. Had Irvine and Rutherford been fit throughout they would surely have won the Championship.

Now, in the early spring time, the weather was, as ever, very Scottish: the skies may have been sparkling but the winds were bitterly cold. Inside the rugby clubhouses there was a special warmth, for Scotland are providing their biggest Lions quota since those tours were a nine-month thrash for Empire Loyalist gents. Eight Scots take on the All Blacks – and, with Robertson unlucky to miss out and Irvine and Renwick not wanting to go, it could well have been eleven.

Any year now the Scottish national side is going to explode and nobody else is going to get a look in. Yet their establishment, in rugby terms, is the most traditional, the most careful of all. While all the other international-playing nations have long allowed their teams to be coached, Scotland resisted till the end of the 1970s. Even in recent times they have displayed the frugality of an Edwardian spinster about both their kin and their kit. Why, it wasn't many years ago that their fine lank of a line-out jumper, Peter Stagg, asked desperately to borrow a colleague's black boot polish before a match at Murrayfield. Stagg cleaning his boots? Unheard of! But it was not for smartness's sake, but to black out a hole in one of his already well-darned blue stockings. He painted out the lilywhite gap in his shin and clattered off for the team photograph. He knew he was going to be dropped and did not think a new pair necessary. In the end an un-laughing committee man produced a new pair of socks. Stagg proudly played in them. He received a bill the following Wednesday and was dropped at the end of the season. Again, when the legendary Jock Wemyss played his first game after the War, having been capped before it, he was sternly asked why he did not have his original blue jersey as only one per player was issued in a lifetime . . .

If the olde worlde rituals of Scottish rugby are gradually changing it is no reason that others should. Mine has evolved into a traditional match-morning mingle with the mob in the foyer of the North British Hotel; a long laugh over an early lunch of oysters and Muscadet at the evocative brass and glass Café Royal with Ian Edwards of ITN, then an exhilarating walk to the ground – usually bent almost double, like a crouching hooker,

The South African, Danie Gerber, played for the Barbarians in the spring to remind the British about the lost art of centre-threequarter play – and what they would continue to miss as long as his Government persisted with its apartheid policies.

into the teeth of a gale. Bernard Levin, an old hand at the Edinburgh Festival, once complimented the ancient City architect on inventing hang-gliding before the sport was given a name!

The match lived up to expectations. The bagpipes started as Scotland set off full of steam, but by the end the Barbarians had run amok, winning 26–13, thanks to some audacious running by three visiting guests. There were, first, the two South African centres, the leggy black Errol Tobias and, especially, the rampaging Springbok, Danie Gerber. Even though this was a gala game, no centre-threequarter in the championship had remotely suggested such a mixture of verve and skill, strength and daintiness. The other man to put a match to the day's festive blue touchpaper was the young French 'B' full-back, Lafond. Handsome is as handsome does; he lit his sparklers all over the place. *Sacre bleu!* Where do they find them? First Blanco, the only truly original back in the season's championship, now this Jack-in-the-box. With luck the two might just play together next season . . .

For me, the most poignant moments of a memorable afternoon came at the final whistle. As the youngsters invaded the pitch, Paparemborde's mighty tree-trunk legs carried him away to retirement. He looked very sad. It was his last game of first-class rugby. He had been near to tears with pride in Paris the previous weekend when he attempted to tell me, in English, of the joy the British Barbarian invitation had given him, a humble Béarnais from the hills around Pau. They had invited him once before, but he could not travel as French airports had been closed because of snow. 'The Barbarian way is his way,' repeated a friendly interpreter. 'Playing with like-minded colleagues, celebrating the joy of life and youth makes for an atmosphere full of chivalry, health and memories.' Alas, his captain, Rives, should also have been saying his farewells in Scotland (though I will only believe his retirement when they cut off his legs!) but he was still nursing his 'Welsh' wounds at home.

Another lament of 'Will ye no' come back again?' was for the dashing Border raider, Jim Renwick. Nor, surely, will the incomparable, stream-lined Slattery be seen again on foreign fields; nor, I suppose, the zig-zag flights of Clive Rees; nor Gareth Davies, the long-time heir apparent to Barry John. And can the doughty Aitken have another starring, stirring, season left in him? It would have been inconceivable to suggest a month or two ago, but another Barbarian we might not see again in the international arena is England's once outstanding No. 8, John Scott. He had set his heart on a Lions place, but he spent the afternoon with the jaded look of a shorn Samson.

The British Lions were leaving in haste just four days after the curtain had been rung down at Twickenham and Cardiff respectively, with the two club Cup Finals. Gloucestershire's county championship was now decorated by the Bristol club, who beat Leicester in a fizzing English final, while the Welsh Cup was won by Pontypool whose relentless, resolute forward play did for the fancied Swansea. Both results, in their differing ways, warmed me: shades of my early journalism in Bristol in the 1950s and John Blake's effervescent, acrobatic play – and, earlier this year, my memories of Ray Prosser ranting across the wastes of Pontypool Park: 'This game's all about effing physical fitness, and I'm 'ere to make sure you can't get enough of it!'

Then the Lions flew. Thirty players and half as many hangers-on. There was one alteration to the original party – Lenihan, of Ireland, had a hernia and was replaced by Bainbridge of England. We read thrillers, watched films, dozed and dreamed. What sort of adventure would it be? Eight of the team had been on the last Lions tour, to South Africa in 1980. This would be a very different trek compared with the one to that beleaguered, unhappy land. Was it really four full years ago that I sat, wide-eyed and shirtsleeved, and watched my first-ever Lions Test? Sitting high in the stand I couldn't help myself exulting in the sport, the passion, the humidity, the orange ball bobbling on the turf of yellowy-green concrete, the red shirts, the white faces . . . By the day, as we Brits trekked through the preliminary games towards that show-down with the South African team, a fervent hope increased that the British would have it in them to put it across the dreaded Springboks with panache and style and flair . . . or maybe, more honestly, just to beat them by as many points as possible. I had never so willed a team to win.

They lost. Well beaten, with only Tony Ward, of Ireland, keeping the British in any sort of contention with his kicking. I cannot remember being so mortified by any team's defeat. For that match was played in Capetown at the end of a week of schools 'riots' where – just a few miles down the road from Newlands – black schoolchildren had been shot at by white policemen. It had been a sickening event, even for that sad country. The British press were not allowed even to report the disturbances: our 'work permits' only let us report rugger, we were told. The odd individual British player may have been discomfited and uneasy but, outwardly, put an impassive, sportsman's none-of-my-business face to the tales we told them, of such as the township mother who wailed at us, and wrung her hands over whether her schoolboy sons would make it home for tea past the police-dog cordons; of the Minister of Sport and his admission that, sure, as a cricket fan, he is glad Basil D'Oliveira managed to leave South Africa in the first place; of the priest who told us of his country – 'those who know don't talk, those who talk don't know;' of old, brave Alan Paton who read to us one day high in the lush rolling hills of Natal the last lines from his classic work, *Cry the Beloved Country*: '. . . and when that dawn will come, of our emancipation, from the fear of bondage and the bondage of fear, why, that is a secret.' And he waved us goodbye, three white, rugger-bugger pilgrims, and gave us an avocado each from his garden – then went all the way back to get a fourth for our Zulu driver, whom he suddenly realised had been waiting patiently outside.

My last remembered symbol at the end of that match in rugby-mad South Africa: the sun dropping low behind the terraced, mountain-end at the Newlands stadium as, at the other end, the blotch of silent black faces remained bowed, upset and let down, for the Lions had lost. Black South Africans support White South Africa's opponents as a matter of course. Each end of the pitch is towered over by rugby posts – those two giant capital H's; one for Heaven . . .

This time, thankfully, no such turmoils as those. Now our minds could concentrate only on fun and sport. We were back in the Southern Hemisphere all right – but now in the sweeter airs of New Zealand. Only once in the century – under Carwyn James in 1971 – had the Lions won a series there. The first British 'invasion' had been in 1888 when a combined team of English and Scottish public schoolboys were organised by the cricketers Shaw, Shrewsbury, and Lillywhite, who took a cut of the profits and the travelling 'sponsorships' from private business in London. They were beaten by club sides, but there was no official international match, for the New Zealand Rugby Union was not formed till four years later.

The game had been introduced to the colony by one Charles John Monro, a young tearaway whose early rumbustuousness is belied by the bewhiskered Edwardian solemnity with which he stares out of the gilded portrait frames that hang on most New Zealand rugby clubhouse walls. He was the son of Sir David Monro, the Speaker in the country's first House of Representatives. Young Charles was getting a skimpy education in the South Island settlement of Nelson in 1867, when, at fifteen, his father sent him for a dose of muscular Christianity to England; he spent three years at Christ's College, Finchley, in North London, and played a code of football that originated from Rugby School and William Webb Ellis. He was more enthusiastic, wide-eyed and rustic than his contemporaries, but played for the school's second XV. Three years later he returned to Nelson and persuaded his mates at the local 'Association' club to give a go to his discovery of this 'hacking and handling' game. Within a year they had crossed Cook Strait to the capital city, where they played a match against fifteen young men of Wellington. Suddenly, these far-away farmers had found other flocks to kill.

The game spread like a bush fire. Within weeks, the Wellington lads had challenged their North Island neighbours, Wanganui – and, appropriately, that's where the 1983 British Lions were booked to sleep off their jet lag. The whitewashed, bungalow, riverside little city was ready with its hospitality as we 'invaders' hit town. The players were transported in a motorcade of vintage cars from the airport after a Maori reception. Lace curtains fluttered behind windows that bore notices 'Welcome to the Lions'. The odd modern car hooted, then galloped away, sheepish and shy.

The main local paper headline was simply 'Our friendly welcome'. Inside were three full pages of rugger stories and photographs. It will be the same here till Saturday. It will be the same everywhere till the tour is over. All the British soccer news, too, with the League tables in full. On

Fitzgerald's line-out throwing through the year was erratic. When it was good, it was very good, when it was bad it was horrid. Here at Cardiff he seeks out Keane and Lenihan. In New Zealand, the French referee, Palmade, cruelly excused the captain's wonky aim. 'It is not deliberate: he is simply mal-co-ordinated.'

the second day we swiped at golf and might have been thousands of miles away, playing at Cheltenham or Hayward's Heath, for we were, as New Zealand's first poet, Pember Reeves, wrote many autumns ago, surrounded by:

> '. . . Smells, sweet English, every one
> And English turf to tread upon,
> And English blackbird's song.'

The new-minted young men from Britain laughed and settled in. All is still serene enough. But up in those green-black hills, hale, grisly, hard-nosed farmers have fenced their sheep from walkabouts and now are packing their black jerseys and preparing to journey down. Their forefathers were more than likely Scottish Border shepherds (as Jim Telfer's certainly were). The breed has been brought up to go to bed early, to get up early, to have its porridge hot and keep its powder dry. It's going to be intriguing to see how Telfer's team respond.

The coach is an appealing man who gets up early as if he owes it to the day. At home he has to – the Selkirk schoolmaster also owns a hotel. He never played a less than honest game for Scotland or the Lions – he was in the British side here in 1966. After the travellers' first night of the long sleep, Telfer was invariably up the earliest, waiting after breakfast in his red tracksuit, clipboard and stopwatch at the ready, to put his boys through the hoop – to sweat fitness into them. The best story to explain the flinty quietness and engaging dour humour of the Lowlander was told me in the winter by the Scottish journalist, Norman Mair. An aspiring coach once showed Telfer with pride the innumerable ploys and strategies he had worked out for his team at kick-offs. Telfer narrowed his eyes and growled: 'Personally, ah dinna like sides which kick-off more than once.'

Suddenly it had become Telfer's team. Willie-John McBride was the front man – the administrator and public relations officer.

'Players in the UK are not used to being highlighted by the media as much as All Blacks are here, and I intend to protect them,' said Willie-John in his bold Ulster voice. (It's like hearing Dr Paisley in his pulpit with your hearing aid turned down.) 'I expect,' he demanded of us, 'you media people to act in a responsible manner.' The big, bland Irishman had decided to keep his boys under wraps. Too much so, thought some old-hand pressmen.

In less than a week Willie-John worked up quite a head of hot air. At the Rotary Club lunch after only four days he told the solid, be-suited merchants that 'Rugby itself had been the success of the last Springbok tour to New Zealand.' That's nonsense: even Rotarians knew it horrendously divided the country right down the middle. Families stopped talking to each other. Legendary figures in the game like Mourie and Robertson refused to play and were martyred or vilified. McBride was then reported to have gone on, obscurely, about something which he called only 'that element'. He said: 'I think New Zealand in many ways came of age during the Springbok tour . . . for New Zealand probably realised for the first time that we have that element living among us. I think that element lives throughout the world today and we must be careful about it.' And then, bless us and save us, Willie was on the wireless again next morning, sagely solving the world economic depression and telling the nation that New Zealand and Northern Ireland would both be okay because they were both food producers. Well, I suppose Ballymena bank workers do understand these things.

Meanwhile the captain, Fitzgerald, kept his pudding-basin haircut below the ramparts. Engagingly he explained: 'I have come on this trip rather as Antony first visited Cleopatra's tent: in other words, not to talk much.'

That was the evening after the opening match in which the local Wanganui side were well – if not flamboyantly – beaten 47–15. It was an error-laden, ball-bobbling game but at least it gave half the squad a stretch. Most hadn't played for weeks. The next match, against mighty Auckland, would be a test all right. This tour was shorter than most – and allowed less time for visitors to play themselves in. And sure enough, they were well and truly clobbered, if only by 13–12.

It was good to be there, as 45,000 Aucklanders took off a midweek Wednesday (on the way, no doubt, to Grandma's funeral) to help tweak the old Lion's tail. The congregation's delight at the winning score was a joy to see. For all their boasting through the week, every extravagant forecast of Auckland's forthcoming victory was tinged with insecurity and doubt. They are Caledonian settlers these and, as in Wanganui, we were played in by yet another swirling pipe band – this one in the routine travelling-rug red and green of the hunting Menzies. Their strangulated Scottish colonial bleats made the heavens open and the first half was played through either horizontal hail or vertical cats'n'dogs. At half time the sun blazed. Then the most bold and lovely of primary sharp rainbows arched over the ground. The crock of gold at the end of it was for the rugby players of Auckland. Dead right too.

There could have been no complaints had Auckland's score been doubled. At the whistle, grey, elderly followers admitted they could not recall a Lions pack anywhere being so outplayed as this one was in the second half – certainly not since Campbell-Lamerton's ultimately bedraggled boys back in 1966.

The British had started well enough, with a presumptuous calm and even boldness. The pack seemed tight and knit, Bainbridge was jumping well, and Holmes was Holmes and Campbell was Campbell. Irwin scored a try and the Lions led 12–6 at the interval.

Yet, by the hour, those two, long, white All Blacks, Haden and Whetton, were gobbling everything in the line-out as if they were beach-boy Joel Garners languidly scrumping coconuts. By the end the Lions eight was out-jumped, out-shoved, out-thought and out-run.

Jeavons of England on the burst. Jilly Cooper's 'body beautiful' was called up for the Lions where he joined (right to left) Beattie, Boyle and Bainbridge.

Somehow, though, they held out, conceding just one try, till the final seconds, when Fox dropped a famous and deserving winning goal.

The Lions were none too dejected as, next day, we switch-backed south by coach, up and down the gravelly, asphalt slalom that leads to Rotorua, skirting misted mountains and scattering a few of the million white dots of mutton that speckle every hillside. There is a decided pong about Rotorua, as if the All Blacks had decided to greet us with stink bombs. It's because the town is ringed by sulphurous geysers and hot springs. It stands on the rim of a steaming lake. Anywhere you look on terra firma can suddenly, from the minutest orifice in the ground, steam up before your eyes. Even in the main street, if the weather's right. Thousands of individual little kettles boiling away – and they still can't make a decent cup of tea!

Telfer had the players quickly on to the practice pitch. It was still early days. He and McBride had numerous options up their sleeves. Might they be as confident as they seem? Might they really be hatching something? We never knew, but we suspected they were playing it straight down the middle. Even so, it was enough to keep the All Blacks' selectors guessing. For all their bravado-tinged-by-insecurity those worthies – a brand-new panel this year – funked naming their Test side for a further week. It was due while we were in Rotorua. Are the All Blacks panicking? Or are they trying to con Willie-John? It's all part of the fun.

Anyway, when it comes I'll be interested to see if it's really true that New Zealand Radio play solemn music from a neighbouring antechamber throughout the day the three selectors are in conclave choosing their XV. Every five minutes, apparently, they go over to the reporter who intones, in hushed voice: 'Still no news, I'm afraid, but we'll interrupt the music the very moment we have any.' All day sometimes. Once, when they were in such a flap about Carwyn James's 1971 team, the chairman of selectors finally emerged, read the team – and someone ran out of the crowd and clocked him on the jaw. Carwyn obviously revelled in such intrigues and passions. I can see him now, taking a long drag at his Senior Service, his eyes twinkling through the smokescreen, and readjusting his twitch of a smile to deadpan. The New Zealanders loved him grudgingly, but couldn't make him out – though not a day has gone past here without at least one person remembering him with sadness and warmth.

Just before he died Carwyn told me of the first of his many tricks to ruffle the New Zealanders. The Lions had lost an early, jet-lagged match in Australia. The following weekend Carwyn was wheeled in by NZTV to watch the highlights of the All Blacks trial game, and to reflect on it in awe.

'In the lowest tones that only a Gwendraeth voice can muster, and on the verge of tears, I said after seeing the film that I would have to re-think my line-out tactics totally. Then I did the unforgiveable. I asked them if they could replay, please, some line-out sequences in which "Meads was battling with the young Peter Whiting".' They didn't find it, of course, because it didn't exist, and Carwyn just went on with the interview – 'but the upshot was that I'd talked Whiting into the Test team and helped the veteran Meads to the captaincy.' Which is just what he wanted!

For all I know McBride and Meads might be up to something similar. But I wonder. Certainly in Rotorua there were a lot of steamy smokescreens wafting around.

The British put up a few signals themselves after beating the local Bay of Plenty side 34–16. Early on there was a crazed bout of fisticuffs, the packs going for each other with all the jerky vim of some truncheoning Keystone Cops. At least two players on each side should have been sent off, certainly Bainbridge and Squire, the captain of the day, who set about Cameron in their own private brawl twenty yards from the rest of the battle. 'We are not here to be intimidated by anyone,' insisted Willie-John at the end.

That, for the moment, was it. Did 'we are not going to be intimidated' mean the Lions were officially allowed to retaliate? Willie-John kept his own counsel on that one. Yet if other ball games took the attitude that retaliation was allowed by the rules we might as well all go home and play pontoon. Soccer is much maligned by rugger men as being played by hooligans from the lower orders, but the standards of refereeing and players' civility and discipline seem set on a far more orderly, even more chivalrous, plane than in rugby union. For McBride to suggest that there is an explicit rulebook allowance for 'justifiable retaliation' is foolhardy – especially when many parents of schoolboys are deeply worried about other more accidental, physical injuries their rugby-playing sons may be prone to. Anyway, I doubt if Willie-John has uttered his last word on the subject. As he spoke, a nice, grudgingly-Scottish smile came from Jim Telfer. On the 1966 Lions tour Jim was captain for the day against Canterbury. Fists flew. Jim had to make the after-match speech. He stood up. 'It was,' he started, 'a very dirty game.' Then he paused. 'Come to think of it, every game in New Zealand is a very dirty game.' He sat down. The end.

By the time the Lions had beaten Wellington 27–19 four days later – another ragged performance by the acclimatising side, relieved by their grit and stamina – a story had broken offering far wider ramifications than a fistfight in the Bay of Plenty. The London *Daily Mail* re-glossed an old 'revelation' that 208 leading players around the world – including twenty of the Lions – had signed contracts for a secretive Australian entrepreneur, David Lord, to take part in a series of professional matches over the next two years. Rumours of the individual rewards varied from £20,000 to £50,000. The players kept mum and laced their boots, the press pirouetted crazily, the tour management pleaded total ignorance and, from far away, Twickenham announced that the Rugby Union committee might discuss the matter at a meeting next month.

The Lions' performance against Wellington did not suggest much mileage for Mammon. If Mr Lord had been watching it would surely have scuppered his plans to show off twenty of them. Circuses need fierce lions – and the Australian cloak-and-dagger merchant would have realised that he had his hand up for a pretty shop-soiled lot.

I still wouldn't be surprised, despite the latest 'certainty' of the revealing source, that this is yet another floater to see how potential sponsors react. This story has been kicking around for a long time – and its perpetrators are showing none of the dash or devil-may-care, let alone the certainty of Mr Packer a few years ago. It is a phoney – not to say funny – situation on tour. The management, of course, deny all knowledge, even though it is an open secret that various groups of players met specially commissioned representatives – each one a recent international player – in Wales, Scotland, Ireland and the north of England in the late winter. Even Twickenham cannot bridle at that: there is nothing wrong in seeing what's on offer. However, judging from whispered nudge-nudge, wink-wink, say-no-mores, a number of players have put their signatures to a legal document. Simply the fact of signature, 'an agreement' to turn professional, will ban them from the Union if International Board rulings are enforced.

Thus, if the names of the twenty 'turncoats' were published during this tour they would be on the next plane home – and at their own expense. If I know my rugger-buggers that, for starters, would be a fairly hefty personal bill for Mr Lord, if he hasn't organised any sponsors yet.

Meanwhile Willie-John sees no evil, hears no evil and speaks in platitudes of total innocence. 'Have they chosen a manager yet?' he asked in defusing jest. Two winters ago the England cricket team were thrown out of Guyana for a breach of the Gleneagles Convention. They were delicate, diplomatic days for the manager, Alan Smith. I wonder how McBride would have handled that. Everyone knew that most of his players had been approached, yet here he was pleading complete ignorance. No, he certainly would not be telephoning London to see what the score was, and he saw no reason why they should phone him. Of course, they hadn't given any thought to a possible twenty replacements. 'I come,' said the big Ulsterman, 'from a country where rumour is rife, and where rumour is part of life. The other week at home I heard someone complaining: "you can't even believe the lies you hear these days." '

So that remains that – until, presumably, Mr Lord can raise his sponsors' loot and his television lucre. Till then – or till someone dares to name names – players will continue to look you in the eye and say: 'Dunno what on earth you're on about.' Mind, Ciaran Fitzgerald was certainly believable when he said, 'Well, nobody has ever approached me. I'm obviously well down on the list.' Mr Lord obviously knew something that the Lions' selectors didn't.

Not that Fitzgerald hadn't played well enough in the victory over Wellington. The bandage round his bullet head was always in the thick of things. His squat little legs whirred him fast about the loose, and he won his share in the tight. His inaccurate line-out throwing remained the worry. Was his pack settling down? It was looking good . . . very good . . . then horrid. The rumbustious, almost veteran Squire was becoming very sharp indeed in the back-row – by far the best of the bunch. The senior locks, Colclough and Norster, were not catching much in the line-outs. Behind the scrum, Holmes and Campbell were suggesting a rewarding partnership – and the wispy Irishman was kicking with exquisite precision. Outside them there was a certain amount of galumph, but little hint, so far, of guile. Cohesive back play had, as yet, been noticeably absent – though the frisky, low-slung Scot, Baird, scored two dasher's tries on this, the capital city's opening fiesta of their winter.

We were spared, for once, in this Caledonian outpost, the squealing Scottish pipe band and were played in instead by an appalling chorus recorded by the Wellington team – 'We're out to whip the Lion/There's no team gamer/Today's the day we do our stuff/Oh, we are the Lion tamer.' There were also a reeling eightsome of extremely inept, very podgy girl cheerleaders, dressed like the Wellington team, in the black and gold of Wolverhampton Wanderers. And indeed the Wolves scavenged well and could easily have won. The brightest thing about the Lions – apart from Baird's bustle and Campbell's kicks – was their jerseys. It's not quite the scarlet of Llanelli or Wales, more the rich red of an over-preserved strawberry jam.

There was still a lot of work to be done. Even if half the team had contracts in their pockets they were still playing like a bunch of amateurs. We were little less than a week away from the first Test match: in a series of four, the first is always the most crucial.

'Well I was a bit surprised, too, but Willie John's Gran was already out here . . .'

CHAPTER ELEVEN

'By Sticking Together, We'll Keep on the Leather'

It goes without saying that the crowds have flocked to watch the Lions. In quaint, friendly New Zealand – where church is low, tea is high and brows are middling – rugby football is the enduring passion. Even in the little grid-square market towns which they call cities – like Rotorua or, where the Lions camp before flying to Christchurch for the Test match, Palmerston North – have their rugby museums. In Rotorua it is a touching little affair. At the back of a sport's outfitters you have to pay a dollar to duck behind a curtain and enter the carpeted, soft-musaked sanctum. It's mostly old programmes and club-housey, glass-cased, venerable jerseys. Nothing as riveting as Bob Scott's toupee, or Mr Kelleher's whistle (or even his right arm) with which he sent off Colin Meads at Murrayfield.

But there were photographs of Barry John opening the 'Barry John Hotel' (it's now called 'The Thermal') in 1971, and there's Terry Cobner's Pontypool shirt looking so tattered that he might have taken on the 5th cavalry in it (which in a way he did). There, too, is enshrined the Stradey programme and a scarlet shirt, badged with 'Cymru am Byth', from the day they showed the mighty 'Blacks what for.

At Palmerston North the museum is altogether a ritzier job. It is set back from the main road, one storeyed wood and brick, and surrounded by nail-scissored lawns and trim shrubs. It might be a crematorium in Surrey – except for the sounds of the hymn that seeps through the stained-glass window. To the tune *Bless 'em all!*:

> 'Some talk of cricket and some of lacrosse,
> And some of the huntsman's loud call.
> But where can be found
> Such a musical sound
> As the old rugby cry –
> On the Ball!
> By sticking together, we'll keep on the leather
> And sing as we go –
> On the Ball!'

'By Sticking Together, We'll Keep on the Leather'

And so on, till the tape's rewound. That was written by a Palmerston-ian, E. G. Secker, in 1885 – only fifteen years after the first game of rugby was played in New Zealand. That was when Charles Monro finished his schooling at Christ's College, Finchley, and returned to his parents' home in Nelson. Only eighteen years after that, in 1888, the first New Zealand tour to England took place – all Maoris – and the museum caption under the sepia team group said they had performed with 'vigour, pace, initiative, good football sense and abundant good humour.'

Davy Gage was their leading light. He played in sixty-eight of the incredible *seventy-four* games on the tour – Oxford and Cambridge first teams were challenged on successive days, and sometimes five matches were played a week. On that tour the 'Haka' war dance was first performed. When Gage died, friends paid for a gravestone. The inscrip-tion said nothing more than 'He Played for New Zealand'. As the museum curator, John Sinclair, told me with solemnity: 'Those five words say it all. What more can a man aspire to?'

Sinclair scavenges the world for his memorabilia. Unlike cricket, rugby has never been any sort of collector's item. But he has found some souvenirs – a picture, a shirt, a boot . . . to mark all the major tours. After that astonishing Maori pioneering, a touring British side in 1904 won handsomely all their thirteen games in Australia, then travelled across the Tasman Sea to be surprisingly well beaten twice in New Zealand. In the following year, a full, official, mixed-race New Zealand team visited Britain. They were given no chance. On the way over, their steamship almost foundered off Cape Horn, being saved only by the team helping to stoke the boilers for two successive days with a desperate, unending gusto. They docked at Plymouth and at once played Devon, who were expected to roll them over with ease. The result was 55–4. The Fleet Street news agencies did not believe it and changed the information to Devon 55, New Zealand 4. When confirmation came that the visitors had indeed been victorious Fleet Street was still certain the score could only have been 5–4, which was the result they released for second editions.

Then continued a trail of runaway victories around the land. They played in black shirts, but their nickname remained 'The Kiwis'. In their sixth game at Hartlepool – then a stronghold of the Union game – they won 63–0, and a leading London writer of the day, a Mr Vivian, tried to explain before the match that the secret of the upstarts' game was based on each man being very fit, fast and athletic, unlike the British tradition of lumbering, butterfingered forwards, and darting, dainty backs. Pro-nounced Vivian: 'They are all backs.' When the billboard announcing this legend was sent up with the newspaper train to Hartlepool, the local newsagent could not understand it. But he knew the colour of the tourists' shirts. He changed all the billings to 'They are all blacks.' The name stuck – as did another for that same mesmerising colonial team of 1905: 'The Originals'.

The Maoris continued to take to the game with a will. There was never any suggestion of anything but mixed-race teams or games – until the dreaded South Africans dipped in their whitewood oar. It remains as New Zealand's eternal shame that the New Zealand Rugby Board agreed not to pick any Maoris for their 1919 tour to Yarpieland. That, as the museum diarist notes, 'set an unfortunate precedent for our subsequent tours of that country'. The Maoris, as a solo team, have yet, of course, to tour South Africa. A Maori side did play the Springbok tourists to New Zealand in 1929. At Napier. This is what the travelling correspondent for the South African newspaper group, E. H. W. Blackett, filed back home – 'It is one thing to organise a football match between Blacks and White people, but quite another to witness Whites in New Zealand cheering on a team of Blacks. It was horrifying.'

The only time the New Zealanders played in white was at home in 1930, the first time the British Lions were so named on Twickenham's headed notepaper. Again a journalist had inspired it – when a British side had attempted to maul the 'Springboks' of South Africa two years before. In 1930, ninety-seven British players were approached before a final party of twenty-nine could be assembled. Not many could take off two-thirds of a year for however stimulating an adventure. It was only on the eve of the team's departure from Southampton that the Leicester international, F. D. Prentice, was told to captain the side – and he was presented with a laundry hamper containing thirty royal blue shirts, each crested by three gilt lions rampant. So when the game began the All Blacks changed to white. By 1950 the mother country wore red. It made no difference – the Brits were trampled underfoot again. Now, more than fifty years on, the boys in black are down from their green-grey, sheep-speckled hills to stifle another invasion from the Redcoats.

I suppose the most dramatic curio in the collection at Palmerston North remains the famous menu note to Billy Wallace, insisting that 'Deans did score at Cardiff' – following the celebrated incident when the All Blacks were, they still insist, robbed of their winning try in 1905. They say the Welsh pulled him back from the try line. There it is, in fading scrawl, and addressed to 'Carbine', which was the racehorse of the day and the nickname for Wallace – rather like Derek Randall being called Arkle. For the rest, there are casefuls of club jerseys so oddly beloved by rugger enthusiasts: old press pix and long-forgotten match programmes; Don Clarke's square-toed right boot, and also, for some unearthly reason, Delme Thomas's left boot. I suppose it was too painful for them to ask for Barry John's! Like Graumann's at Hollywood, there are no end of footprints and palm-casts – of Dawes and Gibson and Meads and Scott and Going and the best of all the Bee-Gees – the Maori winger, Bryan Williams. There is a portrait in oils of Tony O'Reilly; a red tasselled Welsh international cap from the turn of the century, badged with crossed leeks; a letter from the Queen; and a display of nails, glass splinters and fishing hooks picked off the field that the Springboks were due to play on two years ago . . .

And you come out humming the tune of *Bless 'em All*! –

'By sticking together, we'll keep on the leather.
And sing as we go –
On the Ball!'

They went for more than the leather later in the day. The Lions beat the locals of Manawatu 25–18, but Fitzgerald and Paxton ended up with cuts – from kicks, they said. 'Only the fellow who did it knows if it was deliberate,' said McBride at the end of the scatty, error-smudged, wind-blown match. Truthfully, I hadn't noticed the two alleged 'stamping' incidents, but the heads were cut for sure. On the television replays they were more evident. Fitzgerald later called the local culprit 'a coward'. I wondered if Willie-John's sombre sadness – 'Such things would never be tolerated in British rugby' – was a warning to the referee for Saturday's Test match. For the first time in the historic fixtures in New Zealand a neutral referee would administer the internationals – the first two would be taken by Francis Palmade, the respected French official. The trouble was a difference in interpretation: in New Zealand it was 'manly' to be seen as playing an over-robust game – in Europe, referees expected not to have to turn a blind eye, but for players to be more cunning or, if you like, sly. Palmade had a reputation as a disciplinarian. He had a distinctive refereeing style: he liked to take up some odd positions, often quite a distance from the ball. But to my mind he did not miss much. Perhaps Willie-John was displaying some cunning, I thought, as we scribbled down his objections to New Zealand forward play.

When does Monsieur Palmade hit town? Okay lads, let's keep the story boiling till he does. On the eve of the match rugby's Inspector Clouseau will sit in his hotel bedroom and he won't need a dictionary to get the drift of such headlines as 'Lions Roar Over Stamping' or 'McBride Slams NZ Rucking' or 'British Cry Cheats' or, best of all, to appeal to a trim, gentlemanly and courteous Frenchman, 'NZ Methods Not European, Says Angry McBride'.

By next Saturday things will be bubbling, but meanwhile the locals have good reason to laugh all the way to the next ruck: Willie-John was one of the most combative forwards ever to wear a Lions jersey. At the celebrations after the match another old warrior was told of McBride's outburst on dirty play. Colin Meads, probably the most rugged, most trenchant All Black forward of them all, affected a slow-burning, almost nostalgic yearning roll of his eyes. He smiled momentarily, but know-ingly. 'That's rich,' he said, 'coming from the fellow who once almost broke my rib-cage.'

The two had first come across each other twenty years ago: Ireland v All Blacks on the 1963 tour. The game wasn't very old when McBride delivered a mean blow to Meads's body. Meads went down. He said he could scarcely move as his captain, Whineray, rushed to him. 'Get up, Piney. Don't let them see you're injured. Get up.' 'Whineray almost had to drag me to the next line-out. He sought out McBride and told him, "total war, McBride." It went on longer than the last two World Wars put together.'

Thus poacher turns gamekeeper. McBride himself almost admits he was no angel. On his retirement he wrote: 'The one lesson the Lions learned in South Africa and New Zealand was that you must stand up to anything that's thrown at you. I constantly reminded the team of my philosophy: "We never step back. Never step back, whether it's a scrum, a line-out, a ruck or a maul." During the third Test a fracas broke out which was probably the turning point of that game. We had to defend ourselves and lashed into them to drive them back some twenty yards. After that there was a scrum and I could feel every Lion saying: "That's it, we never stood back." From then on the game was over for South Africa.'

On Tuesday Mid-Canterbury were beaten easily enough – and the Lions had four days to sharpen their claws. The battle-lines continued to be drawn up as leafy, sleepy Christchurch gathered its prim skirts about itself and listened in horror to pre-Test match verbals about dirty play that have continued since Willie-John slung his wily pigeon into the black cats' home last Saturday. Gleeful gossip, beery bar-room anticipation and po-faced editorials have been flying around. Nothing like a good ol' Pommie winge to get the ol' boy scout-type hats assailing the air. There was one particularly apt letter amid a pile of boring ones in the local press: 'Sir – I wonder how long it will take the Lions to realise that, in Godzone, use of the head to damage an opponent's boot incurs a penalty – Yours, etc'. Incidentally, Godzone is every settler's name for his beloved land.

That outstanding All Black back-row bandit, Murray Mexted, put in his two penn'orth of erudition, being quoted during the week as saying, simply: 'Discipline is Bullshit!' Someone even dredged up the reason that superlative Maori, Waka Nathan, missed three-quarters of the All Black's tour to Britain in 1967. He was 'done', they say, by the present chairman of the England selectors, 'Your old lad-i-dah, Budge Rogers'. Said Nathan: 'It was the fourth match of the trip. We'd been jostling each other at the rear of the line-out – nothing nasty. Then suddenly he punched me, and I knew my jaw was broken.'

Meanwhile Christchurch tried to potter on with its gentle business. If New Zealand is even more British than the British then it seems even more so here. Olde Englande is alive and well in Godzone. The tiny River Avon snakes amiably through the city. On its banks the first settlers' huts were nailed up proudly in the spring of 1851. Now it is flanked by English lawns, and carefree ducks and drakes, and English willows, weeping serenely, and laurels and birch and birdsong. And over the little willow-pattern bridges Austins and Morrises and Vauxhall Victors doodle un-dangerously.

The All Blacks started the week as runaway favourites. At training they look full of glowering menace and skill. But, slowly, I sensed the old insecurities getting a hold of the populace, and now all the folk who were

Irwin lassoed two strides into his one menacing gallop at Christchurch. In this period the Lions manufactured and muffed a number of good chances. They didn't come again.

so aggressively colonial and cocky on Monday are insisting on the eve of the match that the Lions can surely not be underdogs. The Brits at least seem a pretty good muddling-through side. They've won five out of six – with no harmonious conviction, maybe, but almost every time they've managed to get it together at the last. Yet, to all intents, the tour begins and ends here at Christchurch. If the ending is happy Willie-John has promised to go through his full vocal repertoire after the match. He used to be famed for his late night 'singalongabings' – sea shanties and all, 'Irish Eyes', 'Kathleen', 'The Hills of Antrim' and 'Danny Boy'. All he asks is that we hacks find him a bottle of his favourite Tullamore Dew and that the players conjure up a victory. Both in these parts are tall orders.

In the event, I admit I found myself ambivalent. My first and long anticipated Test match in New Zealand summoned up in me nothing like the passionate commitment and anxieties for the British as I remember from the first Lions Test I saw at Cape Town in 1980. Truthfully, I really did want the better team to win this time, the one with the most flair and dynamism.

The pre-match atmosphere was also vastly different from Cape Town. That was South Africa at prayer, South Africa right or wrong. The preliminaries here were simply those of a South Seas knees-up. The police

Price and Colclough shield
Holmes as he whips out
his pass to Campbell. A
few minutes later the
scrum-half hobbled from
the field – and the tour. In
two Lions' trips Holmes
has managed no more
than a handful of games.
Would the rest of the world
ever be able to judge
what Wales have been
boasting about for so long?

band played songs from the shows, and their dogs larked about to order. A Cheerful Charlie MC conducted the hymn-singing from the pitch: 'C'mon! Let's show 'em up there they haven't cornered the choral market at Cardiff and Wimbledon!' I supposed he meant Wembley – but then he went on to exhort his multitude to 'be heard with envy all the way to that Arms Park crowd in Dublin!' The throng of 40,000 sang the rugger song I'd heard at the Palmerston Museum – 'On the ball'. They sang 'God Save the Queen' with a reverent, by-heart, gusto – but for New Zealand's national song they had to read the words from the programme.

Then the Lions came out – and played above themselves. Unless the All Blacks were outrageously below par and nervous. Whatever, the British raised their game wonderfully well. Campbell kicked three goals to Hewson's two, and they led by 9–6 at half-time. The line-outs were not going badly, nor were the set scrums, and in the loose the old hand, Squire, was leading his young back-row colleagues Paxton and Winterbottom on a most unlikely rampage. Yet in the end the Lions blew it. They won ball after ball and did nothing with it. Just on half-time the British backs had two glaring chances, and they squandered them both. I thought then of Fitzgerald's opinion as offered back in the Irish winter – that it was imperative in a close match to score your points in the passages when you are on top. Campbell played a lovely game but, outside him, all was predictable and unpolished. Two more penalties were swapped, then midway through the second-half, after the trace of a forward pass on the right, the All Blacks swung the ball left and Shaw went over. 13–12, and with just two minutes left Hewson dropped a goal to seal an unconvincing home-side victory.

The Lions were shattered. They cursed themselves. Against all predictions, they had the game in their grasp. They got so close, yet failed. They suffered, too, a tragic blow that could even have settled the series. After half an hour their champion, Holmes, badly damaged his right knee in a freak accident – jumping for the ball at the rear of the line-out with, comparatively, no one near him. He was taken to hospital – the ligaments were torn and the capsule, which provides fluid, had burst. It was the second successive Lions tour that has had Holmes leaving, early and wounded, to fly back home to Wales, for even before the first Test in 1980 in South Africa he had damaged the very same knee.

I flew back even before Terry, leaving Christchurch as the guns in the park boomed out their annual salute to signal the Queen's Birthday. My journal, which had started on Armistice Day in Toulouse, was done. From New Zealand's winter I was back for the British high-summer festivals of cricket and tennis and golf. On the Saturday after I landed home I got up on a warm, West Country morning and watched the BBC's live transmission of the second Test at Wellington. It was played in a ferocious gale, but it was the ferocious All Blacks one trembled at. They won 9–0, but the score could have been trebled. The British could not win the series now.

When worlds collide. Black potted by red as Lions winger Trevor Ringland meets the mighty Mexted amidships.

On my first Lions trip, in 1980, the accompanying press party chipped in a few bob each week to give the players a phone call home. On their £5.75-a-day pocket money it was the least we could do. It was also in beleaguered South Africa, so possibly we were more inclined to stick together for the sake of civilised and spiritual home comforts. There had been no such practice on this tour – perhaps through Willie-John's determination to shelter his team from any outside influences and his general suspicion of what he calls 'the press media'; or possibly because the players' expenses have been increased to a daily £8. So my farewell present to just two of the Lions was the price of a phone call home: for Carleton, because he was the only Lancashire cap in the side, and I was the old *Manchester Guardian* – and for Boyle, because he was Gloucester, like me. I hoped it might help the homesickness; at 2–0 down, that might be setting in fast.

Back home, Wimbledon and Lord's and Ascot buzzed with their usual frenzied action. The newspapers recorded everything that moved – only occasionally finding space to report the latest negotiations in a professional Australian's bid to buy out amateur British rugby players, or the most recent challenges issued to the rest of the sporting world from white South Africa . . .

The despatches from New Zealand made increasingly sombre reading. Suddenly the sorry Test tale was compounded by an epidemic of injuries. At Wellington the Lions pack had not even played with the zest they had occasionally mustered in the first Test, for by then the rumbustious all-round qualities of the two Welsh forwards, Stephens at prop and Squire in the back-row, had been seen for the last time. They, too, left for home, and in the Test itself the Scot, Ian Paxton, who had suggested more than a few hints of sterling play, limped away, and though he was to return for the latter week or two by then Norster had gone for good. Melville, the young English scrum-half, had flown out to replace Holmes, played one sparkling match against Southland, and then he too was injured.

That, at least, resulted in a little romantic adenda – for the resulting SOS was answered by one Steve Smith, and he flew out from England on the very day after – with apt and mischievous irony – the sudden resignation was announced of the chairman of the England selectors, Budge Rogers, with whom of course Smith had crossed verbal swords in the winter. So he was a Lion at last – and they made him captain in his very first game, at Hawkes Bay, a remarkable tribute to his qualities as a leader.

Jeavons, of England, had also come out to supplement the wounded, weary bunch. And as the injuries continued so did the flow of replacements. The originally selected lock, Lenihan of Ireland, and his compatriot, McLoughlin arrived – and also, to ballast the back-row, the Welsh captain, Butler. There was also a sudden rumour that the beleaguered Brits would sent for Gloucester's Blakeway, for that worthy had announced he regretted his decision to retire, and was once more ready, willing, and able, for the cause.

In the event, none played any significant part in the remaining Test matches. The New Zealanders, with their settled team, had found a relentless rhythm. Even from a million miles away, it was increasingly apparent that the Lions were simply not good enough to win a Test match. That glimmer of opportunity they had so wantonly squandered in the first match at Christchurch never repeated itself. At Wellington it was not the gale that laid them to waste, one realised, but the stark fact that the British threequarters did not have the confidence or even the technique to spin the ball, whatever the weather. Already, after just two Tests, British back play had been laid to rest. There were going to be some sad – and stern – post-mortems.

A feature of the All Blacks' display at Wellington had been their tight and disciplined control in the second-half – when the British had the raging wind behind them – in not allowing Campbell one kick at goal.

Campbell again clears his waterlogged lines in the third Test, as Paxton and Colclough set off in chase once more. But the New Zealanders were to deny the Irishman even one kick at goal.

Maurice Colclough is surrounded by All Blacks as he attempts to win the ball during the Christchurch Test.

Dalton and Hobbs scrag Winterbottom. Loveridge and Haden wait for the ball to slither free.

This they repeated in the third Test at Dunedin, again spiking the Irishman's lethal armoury. As the tour continued Campbell's potency in every aspect of play was increasingly dampened, though he tackled cleanly and bravely to the last.

The operative word at Dunedin was 'damp'. For three days and nights before the Test it teemed down. Whenever a player fell on the ball it set up a bow wave like a water-skier's slalom turn. The conditions were lamentable; but so were the Lions' tactics. They decided on high, up-and-under punts followed by a squelching charge. The New Zealanders had given much more thought to the conditions. The backs wore mittens for a better grip on the oval lump of soap, while the whole team had on thin, skin-divers' rubber vests. And, most crucially, whenever they won the ball they hacked low, torpedo skidders past the Lions and far into the waterlogged corners. Nevertheless the Lions were twice in the lead. At the very start, the winger Baird scored from a kick-ahead with a swimmer's racing dive in the corner, and in the second half the little Scot did fine work, again in concert with Evans, to give Rutherford a marvellous try and, with it, probably the Lions' most memorable minute of the tour. But the 8-6 lead was short-lived. The New Zealanders calmly kicked for the most flooded Lions' corner, tied themselves to it as if with a hawser to a dockside capstan – and did not relent until the ever-magnificent Loveridge had inspired a try for Wilson. The British left the field wet, bedraggled and well beaten by 15-8.

The final Test match at Auckland was, simply, a humiliation for the British. They were run ragged by a flamboyant home side which, from the kick-off, seemed to treat the occasion as if it were an exhibition game. New Zealand won by 38-6. Another twenty All Blacks' points would not have been undeserved. Fitzgerald's forlorn forwards lost the ball in both set scrums and line-outs by the calamitous ratio of four to one. The handful of occasions the backs had the ball in their hands they were, by all accounts, as inept as we used to be in the Cainscross 3rd XV. At least, wrote Clem Thomas in the *Observer*, the performance 'finally removes the burden borne by the 1966 Lions as being the worst ever British Isles team to visit New Zealand'. That team's worst defeat had been by 20-3.

Afterwards, McBride admitted to the 'worst ever' label. The British he accepted, 'were now exposed as naive in the arts of rugby football'. The

Rival captains and rival hookers, having swapped shirts, leave the field at the end of the third Test. Dalton, left, looks content. 0-3 down and the strain is telling on Fitzgerald.

Carleton, one of the few consistent successes on the tour, is just too late to stop Fraser hacking on as New Zealand begin yet another surging attack at Auckland.

team left for home a chastened lot. The New Zealanders remained the champions of the world.

For a bet during his rampaging captaincy of the Lions in South Africa nine years before McBride, the Ulster Protestant, had promised that if the Lions won the third Test – to give themselves an unassailable 3-0 lead – he would attend Roman Catholic Mass the following day. Amid great good cheer he was up early for the eight-o-clocker next morning. After the British side were so humbled in Auckland I fancied that Willie-John could well have considered getting down on his knees again. This time any church would do. Only the power of prayer can revitalise British international rugby. It will be interesting to see how quickly – if at all – the prayers are answered.

Statistics

" I SEE SELWYN'S STILL TRYING TO CATCH THE EYE OF THE RUGBY CIRCUS CHAP. "

European Teams

15 JANUARY 1983

ENGLAND 15   FRANCE 19

Scorers
ENGLAND   Hare (4 penalties)
Cusworth (drop goal)

FRANCE   Esteve (try)
Sella (try)
Paparemborde (try)
Camberabero (penalty)
Blanco (2 conversions)

ENGLAND   W. Hare; J. Carleton; H. Davies; P. Dodge; A. Swift;
L. Cusworth; S. Smith (captain); C. Smart; P. Wheeler;
G. Pearce; M. Colclough; (sub: R. Hesford); S. Bainbridge;
N. Jeavons; P. Winterbottom; J. Scott.

FRANCE   S. Blanco; P. Sella; C. Belascain; D. Codorniou; P. Esteve;
D. Camberabero; G. Martinez; P. Dospital; P. Dintrans;
R. Paparemborde; J-C. Orso; J. Condom; J-P. Rives (captain);
L. Rodriguez; J-L. Joinel.

Referee   D. Burnett (Ireland)

15 JANUARY

SCOTLAND 13   IRELAND 15

Scorers
SCOTLAND   Laidlaw (try)
Dods (2 penalties)
Renwick (drop goal)

IRELAND   Campbell (3 penalties, conversion)
Kiernan (try)

SCOTLAND   P. Dods; K. Robertson; J. Renwick; D. Johnston; R. Baird;
R. Wilson; R. Laidlaw (captain); G. McGuinness; C. Deans;
I. Milne; W. Cuthbertson; A. Tomes; J. Calder; I. Paxton;
D. Leslie.

IRELAND   H. MacNeill; T. Ringland; D. Irwin; M. Kiernan; M. Finn;
O. Campbell; R. McGrath; P. Orr; C. Fitzgerald (captain);
G. McLoughlin; D. Lenihan; M. Keane; F. Slattery; W. Duggan;
J. O'Driscoll.

Referee   J-C. Yche (France)

5 FEBRUARY

WALES 13   ENGLAND 13

Scorers

WALES	Squire (try)
	Dacey (drop goal)
	Wyatt (2 penalties)
ENGLAND	Carleton (try)
	Hare (2 penalties)
	Cusworth (drop goal)
WALES	M. Wyatt; E. Rees; D. Richards; M. Ring; C. Rees; M. Dacey; T. Holmes; C. Williams; W. James; G. Price; R. Norster; J. Squire; R. Moriarty; D. Pickering; E. Butler (captain).
ENGLAND	W. Hare; J. Carleton; H. Davies; P. Dodge; A. Swift; L. Cusworth; S. Smith (captain); C. Smart; S. Mills; G. Pearce; S. Boyle; S. Bainbridge; N. Jeavons; P. Winterbottom; J. Scott.
Referee	J. West (Ireland)

5 FEBRUARY

FRANCE 19   SCOTLAND 15

Scorers

FRANCE	Esteve (2 tries)
	Blanco (3 penalties, 1 conversion)
SCOTLAND	Robertson (try)
	Gossman (2 drop goals)
	Dods (1 penalty, 1 conversion)
FRANCE	S. Blanco; P. Sella; C. Belascain; D. Codorniou; P. Esteve; C. Delage; P. Berbizier; R. Paparemborde; J. Dupont; P. Dospital; J-P. Rives (captain); J-C. Orsco; J. Condom; J-L. Joinel; L. Rodriguez.
SCOTLAND	P. Dods; K. Robertson; J. Renwick; D. Johnston; R. Baird; B. Gossman; R. Laidlaw (captain); J. Aitken; C. Deans; I. Milne; W. Cuthbertson; A. Tomes; J. Calder; J. Beattie; D. Leslie.
Referee	A. Richards (Wales)

19 FEBRUARY

SCOTLAND 15   WALES 19

Scorers	
SCOTLAND	Renwick (try)
	Dods (3 penalties, 1 conversion)
WALES	Jones (try)
	Rees (try)
	Wyatt (3 penalties, 1 conversion)
SCOTLAND	P. Dods; K. Robertson; J. Renwick; D. Johnston; R. Baird; B. Gossman; R. Laidlaw (captain); J. Aitken; C. Deans; I. Milne; W. Cuthbertson; A. Tomes; J. Calder; J. Beattie; D. Leslie.
WALES	M. Wyatt; E. Rees; D. Richards; R. Ackerman; C. Rees; M. Dacey; T. Holmes; S. Jones; W. James; I. Eidman; S. Perkins; R. Norster; J. Squire; E. Butler (captain); D. Pickering.
Referee	R. Quittenton (England)

19 FEBRUARY

IRELAND 22   FRANCE 16

Scorers	
IRELAND	Finn (2 tries)
	Campbell (4 penalties, 1 conversion)
FRANCE	Blanco (try, 2 penalties, 1 conversion)
	Esteve (try)
IRELAND	H. MacNeill; T. Ringland; D. Irwin; M. Kiernan; M. Finn; O. Campbell; R. McGrath; P. Orr; C. Fitzgerald (captain); G. McLoughlin; D. Lenihan; M. Keane; F. Slattery; J. O'Driscoll; W. Duggan.
FRANCE	S. Blanco; P. Sella; D. Codorniou; C. Belascain; P. Esteve; C. Delage (sub: V. Vivies); P. Berbizier; P. Dospital; B. Herrero; R. Paparemborde; J. Condom; J-F. Imbernon; J-P. Rives (captain); D. Erbani; J-L. Joinel.
Referee	A. Hosie (Scotland)

5 MARCH

WALES 23   IRELAND 9

Scorers
WALES	Wyatt (try, 1 penalty, 1 conversion)
	Holmes (try)
	Rees (try)
IRELAND	Campbell (2 penalties)
	MacNeill (1 penalty)
WALES	M. Wyatt; E. Rees; R. Ackerman; D. Richards; C. Rees; M. Dacey; T. Holmes; S. Jones; W. James; G. Price; J. Perkins; R. Norster; D. Pickering; E. Butler (captain); J. Squire.
IRELAND	H. MacNeill; T. Ringland; D. Irwin; M. Kiernan; M. Finn; O. Campbell; R. McGrath; P. Orr; C. Fitzgerald (captain); G. McLoughlin; F. Slattery; D. Lenihan; M. Keane; J. O'Driscoll; W. Duggan.
Referee	J. Trigg (England)

5 MARCH

ENGLAND 12   SCOTLAND 22

Scorers
ENGLAND	Horton (drop goal)
	Hare (3 penalties)
SCOTLAND	Laidlaw (try)
	Smith (try)
	Robertson (drop goal)
	Dods (3 penalties, 1 conversion)
ENGLAND	W. Hare; J. Carleton; P. Dodge; H. Davies; A. Swift; J. Horton; S. Smith; C. Smart; P. Wheeler; G. Pearce; N. Jeavons; S. Boyle; S. Bainbridge; P. Winterbottom; J. Scott (captain).
SCOTLAND	P. Dods; J. Pollock; J. Renwick; K. Robertson; R. Baird; J. Rutherford; R. Laidlaw; J. Aitken (captain); C. Deans; I. Milne; J. Calder; I. Paxton; T. Smith; D. Leslie; J. Beattie.
Referee	T. Doocey (New Zealand)

19 MARCH

IRELAND 25   ENGLAND 15

Scorers	
IRELAND	Slattery (try)
	Campbell (try, 5 penalties, 1 conversion)
ENGLAND	Hare (5 penalties)
IRELAND	H. MacNeill; T. Ringland; D. Irwin; M. Kiernan; M. Finn; O. Campbell (sub: A. Ward); R. McGrath; W. Duggan; J. O'Driscoll; M. Keane; D. Lenihan; F. Slattery; G. McLoughlin; C. Fitzgerald (captain); P. Orr.
ENGLAND	W. Hare; J. Carleton; C. Woodward; P. Dodge; D. Trick; J. Horton; N. Youngs; J. Scott (captain); P. Winterbottom; S. Bainbridge; S. Boyle; N. Jeavons; G. Pearce; P. Wheeler; C. Smart.
Referee	J. Anderson (Scotland)

19 MARCH

FRANCE 16   WALES 9

Scorers	
FRANCE	Esteve (try)
	Camberabero (drop goal)
	Blanco (3 penalties)
WALES	Squire (try)
	Evans (1 penalty)
	Wyatt (1 conversion)
FRANCE	S. Blanco; P. Sella; D. Codorniou; C. Belascain; P. Esteve; D. Camberabero; G. Martinez; J-L. Joinel; J-P. Rives (captain); J-F. Imbernon; J. Condom; D. Erbani; R. Paparemborde; P. Dintrans; P. Dospital.
WALES	M. Wyatt; E. Rees; R. Ackerman; G. Evans; C. Rees; M. Dacey; T. Holmes; G. Price; W. James; S. Jones; E. Butler (captain); J. Squire; R. Norster; J. Perkins; D. Pickering.
Referee	T. Doocey (New Zealand)

Final Table

	P	W	D	L	F	A	P
Ireland	4	3	0	1	71	67	6
France	4	3	0	1	70	61	6
Wales	4	2	1	1	64	53	5
Scotland	4	1	0	3	65	65	2
England	4	0	1	3	55	79	1

Leading Scorers

		PG	T	C	DG	P
Campbell	(Ireland)	14	1	3	–	52
Hare	(England)	14	–	–	–	42
Blanco	(France)	7	1	4	1	36
Wyatt	(Wales)	8	2	1	–	34
Dods	(Scotland)	9	–	3	–	33
Esteve	(France)	–	5	–	–	20
Squire	(Wales)	–	2	–	–	8
Finn	(Ireland)	–	2	–	–	8
Rees	(Wales)	–	2	–	–	8
Laidlaw	(Scotland)	–	2	–	–	8

Points Breakdown

	PG	T	C	DG	P
Ireland	15	5	3	0	71
France	8	8	4	2	70
Wales	9	7	3	1	64
Scotland	9	5	3	4	65
England	14	1	0	3	55

Lions' Tour Test Matches

4 JUNE   CHRISTCHURCH

NEW ZEALAND 16   BRITISH ISLES 12

Scorers
NEW   Shaw (try)
ZEALAND   Hewson (3 penalties, 1 drop goal)

BRITISH ISLES   Campbell (3 penalties, 1 drop goal)

NEW   A. Hewson; S. Wilson; S. Pokere; W. Taylor; B. Fraser; I. Dunn;
ZEALAND   D. Loveridge; J. Ashworth; A. Dalton (captain); G. Knight;
                 A. Haden; G. Whetton; M. Shaw; J. Hobbs; M. Mexted.

BRITISH ISLES   H. MacNeill; T. Ringland; D. Irwin; R. Ackerman; R. Baird;
                 O. Campbell; T. Holmes (sub: R. Laidlaw); I. Stephens;
                 C. Fitzgerald (captain); G. Price; M. Colclough; R. Norster;
                 J. Squire; P. Winterbottom; I. Paxton.

Referee   F. Palmade (France)

18 JUNE   WELLINGTON

NEW ZEALAND 9   BRITISH ISLES 0

Scorers
NEW   Loveridge (try)
ZEALAND   Hewson (1 penalty, 1 conversion)

NEW   A. Hewson; S. Wilson; S. Pokere; W. Taylor; B. Fraser;
ZEALAND   W. Smith; D. Loveridge; G. Knight; A. Dalton (captain);
                 J. Ashworth; G. Whetton; A. Haden; J. Hobbs; M. Mexted;
                 M. Shaw.

BRITISH ISLES   H. MacNeill; J. Carleton; G. Irwin; M. Kiernan; R. Baird;
                 O. Campbell; R. Laidlaw; G. Price; C. Fitzgerald (captain);
                 S. Jones; R. Norster; M. Colclough; P. Winterbottom; I. Paxton;
                 (sub: J. R. Beattie); J. O'Driscoll.

Referee   F. Palmade (France)

184

2 JULY   DUNEDIN

NEW ZEALAND 15   BRITISH ISLES 8

Scorers
NEW   Wilson (try)
ZEALAND   Hewson (3 penalties, 1 conversion)

BRITISH ISLES Baird (try)
               Rutherford (try)

NEW   A. Hewson; S. Wilson; S. Pokere; W. Taylor; B. Fraser;
ZEALAND   W. Smith; D. Loveridge; G. Knight; A. Dalton (captain);
               J. Ashworth; G. Whetton; A. Haden; J. Hobbs; M. Mexted;
               M. Shaw.

BRITISH ISLES G. Evans; J. Carleton; M. Kiernan; J. Rutherford; R. Baird;
               O. Campbell; R. Laidlaw; G. Price; C. Fitzgerald (captain);
               S. Jones; S. Bainbridge; M. Colclough; J. Calder; I. Paxton;
               P. Winterbottom.

Referee   R. Byres (Australia)

16 JULY   AUCKLAND

NEW ZEALAND 38   BRITISH ISLES 6

Scorers
NEW   Wilson (3 tries)
ZEALAND   Hobbs (try)
               Haden (try)
               Hewson (try, 2 penalties, 4 conversions)

BRITISH ISLES Campbell, Evans (1 penalty)

NEW   A. Hewson; S. Wilson; S. Pokere; W. Taylor; B. Fraser; I. Dunn;
ZEALAND   D. Loveridge; G. Knight; A. Dalton (captain); J. Ashworth;
               G. Whetton; A. Haden; J. Hobbs; M. Mexted; M. Shaw.

BRITISH ISLES G. Evans; J. Carleton; M. Kiernan; D. Irwin; R. Baird (sub:
               R. Ackerman); O. Campbell (sub: H. MacNeill); R. Laidlaw;
               G. Price; C. Fitzgerald (captain); S. Jones; S. Bainbridge;
               M. Colclough; J. O'Driscoll; I. Paxton; P. Winterbottom.

Referee   R. Byres (Australia)

Full Tour Statistics

	PG	C	T	DG	P
Campbell	22	18	1	6	124
Hare	18	17	–	–	88
Carleton	–	–	9	–	36
Baird	–	–	6	–	24
Irwin	–	–	6	–	24
Rutherford	–	–	2	3	23
Evans	1	3	3	–	21
Ringland	–	–	5	–	20

TOTAL POINTS

	PGC	C	T	DG	P
For	44	39	58	12	458
Against	34	18	30	6	276

Index

Index

Index